ALSO BY MICHAEL ONDAATJE

POETRY

The Collected Works of Billy the Kid

There's a Trick with a Knife I'm Learning to Do

Secular Love

The Cinnamon Peeler

Handwriting

A Year of Last Things

PROSE

Coming Through Slaughter

Running in the Family

In the Skin of a Lion

The English Patient

Anil's Ghost

Divisadero

The Cat's Table

Warlight

NONFICTION

The Conversations: Walter Murch and the Art of Editing Film

THE DISTANCE OF A SHOUT

THE DISTANCE OF A SHOUT

Selected Poems

MICHAEL ONDAATJE

ALFRED A. KNOPF
New York
2026

A BORZOI BOOK
FIRST HARDCOVER EDITION
PUBLISHED BY ALFRED A. KNOPF 2026

Published by Alfred A. Knopf, a division of Penguin Random House LLC, 1745 Broadway, New York, NY 10019. Published simultaneously in Canada by McClelland & Stewart, a division of Penguin Random House Canada, and in Great Britain by Jonathan Cape.

Owing to limitations of space, all acknowledgments to reprint previously published material appear on page 223.

LIBRARY OF CONGRESS CATALOGING-IN-PUBLICATION DATA
Names: Ondaatje, Michael, [date] author.
Title: The distance of a shout / Michael Ondaatje.
Other titles: Distance of a shout (Compilation)
Description: First edition. | New York : Alfred A. Knopf, 2026. |
Identifiers: LCCN 2025006644 | ISBN 9780593805015 (hardcover) |
ISBN 9780593805022 (ebook)
Subjects: LCGFT: Poetry.
Classification: LCC PR9199.3.05 A6 2026 |
DDC 811/.54—dc23/eng/20250602
LC record available at https://lccn.loc.gov/2025006644

penguinrandomhouse.com | aaknopf.com

Printed in the United States of America
1st Printing

The authorized representative in the EU for product safety and compliance is Penguin Random House Ireland, Morrison Chambers, 32 Nassau Street, Dublin D02 YH68, Ireland, https://eu-contact.penguin.ie.

Along with years of thanks, this book is dedicated to Stan Bevington of Coach House Press and to Paul Thompson of Theatre Passe Muraille, as well as the essential communities they created for so many of us.

*

The Distance of a Shout *is also dedicated to my older brother, Christopher Ondaatje. We both had lived lives that were uprooted when we were sent—each of us solitary in our early teens—by ship to different schools in England. A decade later he would make his way to Canada alone, and then a few years later he bought me a ticket and persuaded me to join him there, so giving me the essential gift of a new life.*

Before leaving England, he had introduced me to the pleasures of books and music, especially jazz. And for years at parties he would bring out his guitar and sing a Hoagy Carmichael song, 'Huggin' and Chalkin',' and when he got to the last verse I would join in with him.

Thank you for everything, Christopher.

Contents

BURNING HILLS

HANDWRITING

A YEAR OF LAST THINGS

BURNING HILLS

Light

for Doris Gratiaen

Midnight storm. Trees walking off across the fields in fury
naked in the spark of lightning.
I sit on the white porch on the brown hanging cane chair
coffee in my hand midnight storm midsummer night.
The past, friends and family drift into the rain shower.
Those relatives in my favourite slides
reshot from old minute photographs so they now stand
complex ambiguous grainy on my wall.

This is my Uncle who turned up for his marriage
on an elephant. He was a chaplain.
This shy-looking man in the light jacket and tie was infamous,
when he went drinking he took the long blonde beautiful hair
of his wife and put one end in the cupboard and locked it
leaving her tethered in an armchair.
He was terrified of her possible adultery
and this way died happy to the end.
My Grandmother, who went to a dance in a muslin dress
with fireflies captured and embedded in the cloth, shining
and witty. This calm beautiful face
organized wild acts in the tropics.
She hid the milkman in her house
after he had committed murder and at the trial
was thrown out of the court for making jokes at the judge.
Her son became a Q.C.
This is my Brother at six. With his cousin and his sister
and Pam de Voss who fell on a penknife and lost her eye.
My Aunt Christie. She knew Harold Macmillan was a spy
communicating with her through pictures in the newspapers.
Every picture she believed asked her to forgive him,
his hound eyes pleading.

Her husband, Uncle Fitzroy, a doctor in Ceylon,
had a memory sharp as scalpels into his eighties,
though I never bothered to ask him about anything
—interested then more in the latest recordings of Bobby Darin.

And this is my Mother with her brother Noel in fancy dress.
They are seven and eight years old, a hand-coloured photograph,
it is the earliest picture I have. The one I love most.
A picture of my kids at Halloween
has the same contact and laughter.
My Uncle dying at sixty-eight, and my Mother a year later
  dying at sixty-eight.
She told me about his death, the day he died
his eyes clearing out of illness as if seeing
right through the room, the hospital and she said
he saw something so clear and good his whole body
for a moment became youthful and she remembered
when she sewed badges on his track shirts.
Her voice joyous in telling me this, her face light and clear.
(My firefly Grandmother also dying at sixty-eight).

These are the fragments I have of them, tonight
in this storm, the dogs restless on the porch.
They were all laughing, crazy, and vivid in their prime.
At a party my drunk Father
tried to explain a complex operation on chickens
and managed to kill them all in the process, the guests
having dinner an hour later while my Father slept
and the kids watched the servants clean up the litter
of beaks and feathers on the lawn.
These are their fragments, all I remember,
wanting more knowledge of them. In the mirror and in my kids
I see them in my flesh. Wherever we are
they parade in my brain and the expanding stories

connect to the grey grainy pictures on the wall
as they hold their drinks or twenty years later
hold grandchildren, pose with favourite dogs,
coming through the light, the electricity, which the storm
destroyed an hour ago, a tree going down by the highway
so that now inside the kids play dominoes by candlelight
and out here the thick rain static the spark of my match
                                                                        to a cigarette
and the trees across the fields leaving me, distinct
lonely in their own knife scars and cow-chewed bark,
frozen in the jagged light as if snapped in their run
the branch arms waving to what was a second ago the dark sky
when in truth like me they haven't moved.
Haven't moved an inch from me.

Dates

It becomes apparent that I miss great occasions.
My birth was heralded by nothing
but the anniversary of Winston Churchill's marriage.
No monuments bled, no instruments
agreed on a specific weather.
It was a seasonal insignificance.

I console myself with my Mother's eighth month.
While she sweated out her pregnancy in Ceylon
a servant ambling over the lawn
with a tray of iced drinks,
a few friends visiting her
to placate her shape, and I
drinking the life lines,
Wallace Stevens sat down in Connecticut
a glass of orange juice at his table
so hot he wore only shorts
and on the back of a letter
began to write 'The Well Dressed Man with a Beard.'

That night while my Mother slept
her significant belly cooled
by the bedroom fan
Stevens put words together
that grew to sentences
and shaved them clean and
shaped them, the page suddenly
becoming thought where nothing had been,

his head making his hand
move where he wanted
and he saw his hand was saying
the mind is never finished, no, never
and I in my Mother was growing
as were the flowers outside the Connecticut windows.

Letters & Other Worlds

> *'for there was no more darkness for him and,*
> *no doubt like Adam before the fall, he could see in the dark'*

My father's body was a globe of fear
His body was a town we never knew
He hid that he had been where we were going
His letters were a room he seldom lived in
In them the logic of his love could grow

My father's body was a town of fear
He was the only witness to its fear dance
He hid where he had been that we might lose him
His letters were a room his body scared

He came to death with his mind drowning.
On the last day he enclosed himself
in a room with two bottles of gin, later
fell the length of his body
so that brain blood moved
to new compartments
that never knew the wash of fluid
and he died in minutes of a new equilibrium.

His early life was a terrifying comedy
and my mother divorced him again and again.
He would rush into tunnels magnetized
by the white eye of trains
and once, gaining instant fame,
managed to stop a Perahara in Ceylon
—the whole procession of elephants dancers

local dignitaries—by falling
dead drunk onto the street.

As a semi-official, and semi-white at that,
the act was seen as a crucial
turning point in the Home Rule Movement
and led to Ceylon's independence in 1948.

(My mother had done her share too—
her driving so bad
she was stoned by villagers
whenever her car was recognized.)
For fourteen years of marriage
each of them claimed he or she
was the injured party.
Once on the Colombo docks
saying goodbye to a recently married couple
my father, jealous
at my mother's articulate emotion,
dove into the waters of the harbour
and swam after the ship waving farewell.
My mother pretending no affiliation
mingled with the crowd back to the hotel.

Once again he made the papers
though this time my mother
with a note to the editor
corrected the report—saying he was drunk
rather than brokenhearted at the parting of friends.
The married couple received both editions
of *The Ceylon Times* when their ship reached Aden.

And then in his last years
he was the silent drinker,
the man who once a week

disappeared into his room with bottles
and stayed there until he was drunk
and until he was sober.

There speeches, head dreams, apologies,
the gentle letters, were composed.
With the clarity of architects
he would write of the row of blue flowers
his new wife had planted,
the plans for electricity in the house,
how my half-sister fell near a snake
and it had awakened and not touched her.
Letters in a clear hand of the most complete empathy
his heart widening and widening and widening
to all manner of change in his children and friends
while he himself edged
into the terrible acute hatred
of his own privacy
till he balanced and fell
the length of his body
the blood entering
the empty reservoir of bones
the blood searching in his head without metaphor

Billboards

My wife's problems with husbands, houses,
her children that I meet
at stations in Kingston, in Toronto, in London Ontario
—they come down the grey steps
bright as actors after their drugged four-hour ride
of spilled orange juice and comics.
Reunions for Easter-egg hunts.
Kite flying. Christmases.
All this, I was about to say,
invades my virgin past.

When she was beginning
this anthology of kids
I moved blind but for senses,
jutting *faux pas,* terrible humour,
shifted with a sea of persons,
breaking when necessary
into smaller self-sufficient bits of mercury.
My mind a carefully empty diary
till I hit the barrier reef
that was my wife—
                                        there
the right bright fish
among the coral.

With her came the locusts of history—
innuendoes she had missed
varied attempts at seduction
dogs bred and killed
by taxis or brain disease.
Here was I trying to live

with a neutrality so great
I'd have nothing to think about.

Nowadays I get the feeling
I'm in a complex situation,
one of several billboard posters
blending in the rain.

I am writing this with a pen my wife has used
to write a letter to her first husband.
On it is the smell of her hair.
She must have placed it down between sentences
and thought, and driven her fingers round her skull
gathered the slightest smell of her head
and brought it back to the pen.

Bearhug

Griffin calls to come and kiss him goodnight
I yell ok. Finish something I'm doing,
then something else, walk slowly round
the corner to my son's room.
He is standing arms outstretched
waiting for a bearhug. Grinning.

Why do I give my emotion an animal's name,
give it that dark squeeze of death?
This is the hug which collects
all his small bones and his warm neck against me.
The thin tough body under the pyjamas
locks to me like a magnet of blood.

How long was he standing there
like that, before I came?

A Story

for Akash

For his first forty days a child
is given dreams of previous lives.
Journeys, winding paths,
a hundred small lessons
and then the past is erased.
Some are born screaming,
some full of introspective wandering
into the past—that bus ride in winter,
the sudden arrival within
a new city in the dark.
Those departures from family bonds
leaving what was lost and needed.
So the child's face is a lake
of fast-moving clouds and emotions.

A last chance for the clear history of the self.
All our mothers and grandparents here,
our dismantled childhoods
in the buildings of the past.

Some great forty-day daydream
before we bury the maps.

With all the swerves of history
I cannot imagine your future.
Would wish to dream it, see you
in your teens, as I saw my son,
your already philosophical air
rubbing against the speed of the city.

I no longer guess a future.
And do not know how we end
nor where.

Though I know a story about maps, for you.

A Bus to Fez

I was on a bus for six hours to Fez in those early years
in almost silent conversation with a woman
who had often talked me out of things—a change in life,
a foolishness. And as we spoke the bus travelled
from afternoon to midnight, the desert turning cold,
I felt alone, hungry. I must have imagined her
to have someone to talk with.

We roamed through those brief years of friendship,
pausing at what we both remembered—her quiet
hand on my sleeve warning me of a flame, her laugh
across the room at something foolish I was saying.
Or once, after her awkward confession of a betrayal,
acknowledging *'It was the sixties!'*—a time when I
was still naïve, unaware of the secret lives in others.

We approached Fez, our recollections unfinished,
startled by the lateness, our imagined dialogues a dream.
Earlier she'd murmured how gentleness implied suffering.
And my long-ago friend on that swerving night bus
recited into the dark—
'I don't want to confuse the world anymore with songs about love.
They sound like the giant creakings of a wooden ship
that never comes into port these days . . .'
I said nothing. I knew the two of us loved privacy,
had never shared the solitude within ourselves.
'She has a great poem about Eurydice,' she whispered,
'fearing a man's public light, fearing to be brought home,'
as if this were the essential clue to all stories.

A gust of rain entered the windows of our bus
travelling from Marrakesh to Fez. The darkness hiding
us from others. I was imagining journeys
we might have taken during some pause in her life
or mine to a city as unknown as we were to each other
with nothing or perhaps everything between us.
'Yeah, that would have been nice, to travel alongside you,
sometime,' saying this in a thoughtful exaggerated drawl,
inventing the voice to defend the secrets in herself.
'We could have discovered each other wildly, somewhere,
in Carthage, in a strange room, our bed on its rollers
shuddering on bare wood until it hit the wall, with us
hardly knowing where or even who we were.'

She had never spoken that way to me, but in those
never-given-to-us hours beside strangers, truth
needed to be nothing more than a whisper,
the way the wet skin of her shoulder felt private
against mine, damp from the earlier rain.

'Tell me, will you,' she was saying, thoughtfully,
'after all these years, tell me what you think of me.'
Then looking down at my wanting hand—*'Really.'*

The Hour of Cowdust

It is the hour we move small
in the last possibilities of light

now the sky opens its blue vault

I thought this hour belonged to my children
bringing cows home
bored by duty swinging a stick,
but this focus of dusk out of dust
is everywhere—here by the Nile
the boats wheeling
like massive half-drowned birds
and I gaze at water that dreams
dust off my tongue,
in this country your mouth
feels the way your shoes look

Everything is reducing itself to shape

Lack of light cools your shirt
men step from barbershops
their skin alive to the air.
All day
dust covered granite hills
and now
suddenly the Nile is flesh
an arm on a bed.

In Indian miniatures
I cannot quite remember
what this hour means

—people were small,
animals represented
simply by dust
they stamped into the air.
All I recall of commentaries
are abrupt lovely sentences where
the colour of a bowl
a left foot stepping on a lotus
symbolized separation.
Or stories of gods
creating such beautiful women
they themselves burned in passion
and were reduced to ash.
Women confided to pet parrots
solitary men dreamed into the conch.
So many
graciously humiliated
by the distance of rivers

The boat turns languid
under the hunched passenger,
sails
ready for the moon
fill like a lung

There is no longer
depth of perception
it is now possible
for the outline of two boats
to collide silently

Uswetakeiyawa

Uswetakeiyawa. The night mile

through the village of tall
thorn leaf fences
sudden odours
which pour through windows of the jeep.

We see nothing, only
the grey silver of the Dutch canal
where coloured boats
lap like masks in the night
their alphabets lost in the dark.

No sight but the imagination's
story behind each smell
or now and then a white sarong
pumping its legs on a bicycle
like a moth in the headlights

                        and the dogs
who lean out of night
strolling the road
with eyes of sapphire
and hideous body
                        so mongrelled
they seem to have woken
to find themselves tricked
into outrageous transformations,
one with the spine of a snake
one with a creature in its mouth
(car lights rouse them
from the purity of darkness).

This is the dream journey
we travel most nights
returning from Colombo.

The road hugs the canal
the canal every mile
puts an arm into the sea.

In daylight women bathe
waist-deep beside the road
utterly still as I drive past
their *diya reddha* cloth
tied under their arms.
Brief sentences of women
or an ancient man in spectacles
crossing the canal
only his head visible
pulling something we cannot see
in the water behind him.

In the silence of the night drive
you swallow odours
which change each minute—dried fish
swamp, toddy, a variety of curries
and something we have never been able to recognize.
There is just this thick air
and the aura of dogs
in trickster skin.

Though one night we saw
something slip into the canal.
There was then the odour we did not recognize.
The smell of a dog losing its shape.

Sweet Like a Crow

for Hetti Corea, 8 years old

'The Sinhalese are beyond a doubt one of the least musical people in the world. It would be quite impossible to have less sense of pitch, line or rhythm.' —PAUL BOWLES

Your voice sounds like a scorpion being pushed
through a glass tube
like someone has just trod on a peacock
like wind howling in a coconut
like a rusty bible, like someone pulling barbed wire
across a stone courtyard, like a pig drowning,
a *vattacka* being fried
a bone shaking hands
a frog singing at Carnegie Hall.

Like a crow swimming in milk,
like a nose being hit by a mango
like the crowd at the Royal–Thomian match,
a womb full of twins, a pariah dog
with a magpie in its mouth
like the midnight jet from Casablanca
like Air Pakistan curry,
a typewriter on fire, like a spirit in the gas,
like a hundred pappadans being crunched, like someone
trying to light matches in a dark room,
the clicking sound of a reef when you put your head into the sea,
a dolphin reciting epic poetry to a sleepy audience,
the sound of a fan when someone throws *brinjals* at it,
like pineapples being sliced in the Pettah Market
or betel juice hitting a butterfly in mid-air.

Like a whole village running naked onto the street
and tearing their sarongs, like an angry family
pushing a jeep out of the mud, like dirt on the needle,
like eight sharks being carried on the back of a bicycle
like three old ladies locked in the lavatory
like the sound I heard when having an afternoon sleep
and someone walked through my room in ankle bracelets.

White Dwarfs

This is for people who disappear
for those who descend into the code
and make their room a fridge for Superman
—who exhaust costume and bones that could perform flight,
who shave their moral so raw
they can tear themselves through the eye of a needle
this is for those people
who hover and hover
and die in the ether peripheries

There is my fear
of no words   of
falling without words
over and over   of
mouthing the silence
Why do I love most
among my heroes those
who sail to that perfect edge
where there is no social fuel?
Release of sand bags
to understand their altitude—

that silence of the third cross
third man hung so high and lonely
we don't hear him say
his pain, say his un-brotherhood
What has he to do with the smell of ladies,
can they eat off his skeleton of pain?

The Gurkhas in Malaya
cut the tongues of mules

so they were silent beasts of burden
in enemy territories
after such cruelty what could they speak of anyway
And Dashiell Hammett in success
suffered conversation and moved
to the perfect white between the words

This white that can grow
is fridge, bed,
is an egg—most beautiful
when unbroken, where
what we cannot see is growing
in all the colours we cannot see

There are those burned out stars
who implode into silence
after parading in the sky
after such choreography what would they wish to speak of
anyway

Farre Off

There are the poems of Campion I never saw till now
and Wyatt who loved with the best
and suddenly I want 16th-century women
round me devious politic aware
of stepladders to the king

Tonight I am alone with dogs and lightning
aroused by Wyatt's talk of women who step
naked into his bedchamber

Moonlight and barn light constant
lightning every second minute
I have on my thin blue parka
and walk behind the dogs
who slide under the gate
and sense cattle
deep in the fields

I look out into the dark pasture
past where even the moonlight stops

my eyes are against the ink of Campion

Walking to Bellrock

Two figures in deep water.

Their frames truncated at the stomach
glide along the surface. Depot Creek.
One hundred years ago lumber being driven down this river
tore and shovelled and widened the banks into Bellrock
down past bridges to the mill.

The two figures are walking
as if half sunk in a grey road
their feet tentative, stumbling on stone bottom.
Landscapes underwater. What do the feet miss?
Turtle, watersnake, clam. What do the feet ignore
and the brain not look at, as two figures slide
past George Grant's green immaculate fields
past the splashed blood of cardinal flowers on the bank.

Rivers are a place for philosophy but all thought
is about the mechanics of this river is about
stones that twist your ankles
the hidden rocks you walk your knee into—
feet in slow motion and brain and balanced arms
imagining the blind path of foot, underwater sun
suddenly catching the almond-coloured legs
the torn old Adidas tennis shoes we wear
to walk the river into Bellrock.

What is the conversation about for three hours
on this winding twisted evasive river to town?
What was the conversation about all summer—

Stan and I laughing joking going summer crazy
as we lived against each other.
To keep warm we submerge. Sometimes
just our heads decapitated
glide on the dark glass.

There is no metaphor here.
We are aware of the heat of the water, coldness of the rain,
smell of mud in certain sections that farts
when you step on it, mud never walked on
so you can't breathe, my god you can't breathe this air
and you swim fast your feet off the silt of history
that was there when the logs went
leaping down for the Rathbun Lumber Company
when those who stole logs had to leap
right out of the country if caught.

But there is no history or philosophy or metaphor with us.
The problem is the toughness of the Adidas shoe
its three stripes gleaming like fish decoration.
The story is Russell's arm waving out of the green of a field.

The plot of the afternoon is to get to Bellrock
through rapids, falls, stink water
and reach the island where beer and a towel wait for us.
That night there is not even pain in our newly used muscles
not even the puckering of flesh
and little to tell except you won't
believe how that river winds and when you
don't see the feet you concentrate on the feet.
And all the next day trying to think
what we didn't talk about.
Where was the criminal conversation
broken sentences lost in the splash, in wind.

Stan, my crazy summer friend,
why are we both going crazy?
Going down to Bellrock
recognizing home by the colour of barns
which tell us north, south, west,
and otherwise lost in miles and miles of rain
in the middle of this century
following the easy fucking stupid plot to town.

Pig Glass

This is pig glass
    a piece of cloudy sea

nosed out of the earth by swine
and smoothed into pebble
run it across your cheek
it will not cut you

and this is my hand a language
which was buried for years
                touch it
against your stomach

                    The pig glass
I thought
was the buried eye of Portland Township
slow faded history
waiting to be grunted up
There is no past until you breathe
on such green glass
                rub it
over your stomach and cheek

The Meeks family used this section
years ago to bury tin
crockery, forks, dog tags
and each morning
pigs ease up that ocean
redeeming it again
into the possibilities of rust
one morning I found a whole axle

another day a hand crank
but this is pig glass
tested with narrow teeth
and let lie. The morning's green present—
Portland Township jewellery.

A band from the ankle of a pigeon
a weathered bill from the Bellrock cheese factory
letters in 1925 to a dead mother I
disturbed in the room above the tractor shed.
Journals of family love
servitude to farm weather
a work glove in a cardboard box
creased flat and hard like a flower.

A bottle thrown
by loggers out of a wagon
past midnight
explodes against rock.
This green fragment has behind it
the *booomm* when glass
tears free of its smoothness

now once more smooth as knuckle
a tooth on my tongue.
Comfort that bites through skin
hides in the dark afternoon of my pocket.
Snake shade.
Determined histories of glass.

We're at the Graveyard

Stuart Sally Kim and I
watching still stars.
Up there the clear charts,
the systems' intricate branches
which change with hours and solstices,
the bone geometry of moving from there, to there.

And down here—friends
whose minds and bodies
shift like acrobats to each other.
When we leave, they move
to an altitude of silence.

So our minds shape
and lock the transient,
parallel these bats
organizing the air
with thick blinks of travel.
Sally is like grey snow in the grass.
Sally of the beautiful bones
pregnant below stars

The Gate in His Head

for Victor Coleman

Victor, the shy mind
revealing the faint scars
coloured strata of the brain,
not clarity but the sense of shift

a few lines, the tracks of thought

Landscape of busted trees
the melted tires in the sun
Stan's fishbowl
with a book inside
turning its pages
like some sea animal
camouflaging itself
the typeface clarity
going slow blonde in the sun full water

My mind is pouring chaos
in nets onto the page.
A blind lover, don't know
what I love till I write it out.
And then from Gibson's your letter
with a blurred photograph of a gull.
Caught vision. The stunning white bird
an unclear stir.

And that is all this writing should be then.
The beautiful formed things caught at the wrong moment
so they are shapeless, awkward
moving to the clear.

Moving Fred's Outhouse

All afternoon (while the empty drive-in
screen in the distance promises)
we are moving the two-seater
a hundred yards across his garden

We turn it over on its roof,
and over, and as it slowly
falls on its side
the children cheer

Sixty years old and a change in career—
from these pale-yellow flowers emerging
out of damp wood in the roof
to become a room thorough with flight, noise,
and pregnant with the morning's eggs,
a perch for chickens

Two of us. The sweat.
Our hands under the bottom
then the top as it goes
over, through twin holes the flowers,
running to move the roller, shove,
and everybody screaming to keep the dog away
Fred the pragmatist—dragging the ancient comic
out of retirement and into a television series
among the charging democracy of Rhode Island Reds

Head over heels across the back lawn
old wood collapsing in our hands

All afternoon the silent space is turned

Buck Lake Store Auction

Scrub lawn.
                A chained
dog tense and smelling.
50 cents for a mattress. 50 cents
for doors that allowed privacy.

                                A rain-
swollen copy of Jack London
a magazine drawing of a rabbit
bordered with finishing nails.
6 chickens, bird cage (empty),
sauerkraut cutting board

down to the rock
                        trees

Not bothering to look
into the old woman's eyes
as we go in, get a number
have the power to bid
on everything that is exposed.
After an hour in this sun
I expected her to unscrew
her left arm and donate it
to the auctioneer's excitement.
In certain rituals we desire
only what we cannot have.
While for her, Mrs Germain,

this is where the maniacs
of earth select.

Look, I wanted to say,
$10 for the dog
with faded-denim eyes

Loop

My last dog poem.
I leave behind all social animals,
turn to the one
who appears again on roads
one eye torn out and chasing.

He is only a space filled
and blurred with passing—
will fade
to reappear somewhere else.

He survives the porcupine, cars, poison,
fences with their spasms of electricity.
Vomits up bones, bathes at night
in Holiday Inn swimming pools.

And magic in his act of loss.
The missing eye travels up
in a bird's mouth, and into the sky.
Departing family. It is loss only of flesh
no more than his hot spurt across a tree.

He is the one you see at drive-ins
tearing silent into garbage
while societies unfold in his sky.
The bird lopes into the rectangle nest of images

and parts of him move on.

Moon Lines, after Jiménez

Are you going around naked
in the house?

speaking to the moon

from the precise
place of darkness
speaking to
the unnamed woman

The moon has no shoes
undresses itself of cloud
river reflection

In dark rooms
lost men imagine
paths of biography
on their palms

The greatest shipwrecks
are silent
semaphore their bones
through tide
they grow coloured history
wait
for the clock of moon

The abandoned woman
dives through darkness
and then

balances
with the magic fluid of her ear

It is here
it is now
when my thumb
swallows the candlelight

Late Movies with Skyler

All week since he's been home
he has watched late movies alone
terrible one-star films and then staggering
through the dark house to his bed
waking at noon to work on the broken car
he has come home to fix.

21 years old and restless
back from logging on Vancouver Island
with men who get rid of crabs with Raid
    2 minutes bending over in agony
    and then into the showers!

Last night I joined him for *The Prisoner of Zenda*
a film I saw three times in my youth
and which no doubt influenced me morally.
Hot coffee bananas and cheese
we are ready at 11.30 for adventure.

At each commercial Sky
breaks into midnight guitar practice
head down playing loud and intensely
till the movie comes on and the music suddenly stops.
Skyler's favourite hours when he's usually alone
cooking huge meals of anything in the frying pan
thumbing through *Advanced Guitar* like a bible.
We talk during the film
and break into privacy during commercials
or get more coffee or push
the screen door open and urinate under the trees.

Laughing at the dilemmas of 1890s heroes,
suggestive lines, cutaways to court officials
who raise their eyebrows at least two inches
when the lovers kiss . . .
only the anarchy of the evil Rupert of Hentzau
is appreciated.
                    And still somehow
by 1.30 we are moved
as Stewart Granger girl-less and country-less
rides into the sunset with his morals and his horse.
The perfect world is over. Banana peels
orange peels ashtrays guitar books.
2 a.m. We stagger through
into the slow black rooms of the house.

I lie in bed fully awake. The darkness
breathes to the pace of a dog's snoring.
The film is replayed to sounds
of an intricate blues guitar.
Skyler is Rupert then the hero.
He will leave in a couple of days
for Montreal or the Maritimes.
In the movies of my childhood the heroes
after skilled swordplay and moral victories
leave with absolutely nothing
to do for the rest of their lives.

from The Collected Works of Billy the Kid

In Boot Hill there are over 400 graves. It takes
the space of 7 acres. There is an elaborate gate
but the path keeps to no main route for it tangles
like branches of a tree among the gravestones.

300 of the dead in Boot Hill died violently
200 by guns, over 50 by knives
some were pushed under trains—a popular
and overlooked form of murder in the west.
Some from brain haemorrhages resulting from bar fights
at least 10 killed in barbed wire.

In Boot Hill there are only 2 graves that belong to women
and they are the only known suicides in that graveyard

*

Not a story about me through their eyes then. Find the beginning, the slight silver key to unlock it, to dig it out. Here then is a maze to begin, be in.

Two years ago, Charlie Bowdre and I criss-crossed the Canadian border. Ten miles north of it ten miles south. Our horses stepped from country to country, across low rivers, through different colours of tree green. The two of us, our criss-cross like a whip in slow motion, the ridge of action rising and falling, getting narrower in radius till it ended and we drifted down to Mexico and old heat. That there is nothing of depth, of significant accuracy, of wealth in the image, I know. It is there for a beginning.

*

Mmm mm thinking
moving across the world on horses
body split at the edge of their necks
neck sweat eating at my jeans
moving across the world on horses
so if I had a newsman's brain I'd say
well some morals are physical
must be clear and open
like diagram of watch or star
one must eliminate much
that is one turns when the bullet leaves you
walk off see none of the thrashing
the very eyes welling up like bad drains
believing then the moral of newspapers or gun
where bodies are mindless as paper flowers you dont feed
or give to drink
that is why I can watch the stomach of clocks
shift their wheels and pins into each other
and emerge living, for hours

*

With the Bowdres

She is boiling us black coffee
leaning her side against the warm stove
taps her nails against the mug
Charlie talking on about things
and with a bit the edge of my eye
I sense the thin white body of my friend's wife

Strange that how I feel people
not close to me
as if their dress were against my shoulder
and as they bend down
the strange smell of their breath
moving across my face
or my eyes
magnifying the bones across a room
shifting in a wrist

*

When I caught Charlie Bowdre dying
tossed 3 feet by bullets giggling
at me face tossed in a gaggle
he pissing into his trouser legs in pain
face changing like fast sunshine o my god
o my god billy I'm pissing watch
your hands
                    while the eyes grew all over his body

Jesus I never knew that did you
the nerves shot out
the liver running around there
like a headless hen jerking
brown all over the yard
seen that too at my aunt's
never eaten hen since then

*

I have seen pictures of great stars,
drawings which show them straining to the centre
that would explode their white
if temperature and the speed they moved at
shifted one degree.

Or in the East have seen
the dark grey yards where trains are fitted
and the clean speed of machines
that make machines, their
red golden pouring which when cooled
mists out to rust or grey.

The beautiful machines pivoting on themselves
sealing and fusing to others
and men throwing levers like coins at them.
And there is there the same stress as with stars,
the one altered move that will make them maniac.

*

Sallie Chisum had lived in that desert house fourteen years, and every year she demanded of her uncle John that she be given a pet of some strange exotic breed. Not that she did not have enough animals. She had collected several wild and broken animals that, in a way, had become exotic by their breaking. Their roof would have collapsed from the number of birds who might have lived there if the desert hadn't killed three-quarters of those that tried to cross it. Still every animal that came within a certain radius of that house was given a welcome, the tame, the half-born, the wild, the wounded.

I remember the first night there. John took me to see the animals. About 20 yards away from the house, he had built vast cages, all in a row. They had a tough net roof over them for the daytime when they were let out but tended to stay within the shade of their cages anyway. That night John took me along and we stepped off the porch, left the last pool of light, down into the dark. We walked together smoking his long narrow cigars, with each suck the nose and his moustache lighting up. We came to the low brooding whirr of noise, that night sleep of animals. They were stunning things in the dark. Just shapes that shifted. You could peer into a cage and see nothing till a rattle of claws hit the grid an inch from your face and their churning feathers seemed to hiss, and a yellow pearl of an eye cracked with veins glowed through the criss-crossed fence.

One of the cages had a huge owl. It was vast. All I could see were its eyes—at least 8″ apart. The next morning, however, it turned out to be two owls, both blind in one eye. In those dark cages the birds, there must have been twenty of them, made a steady hum all through the night—a noise you heard only if you were within 5 yards of them. Walking back to the house it was again sheer silence from where we had come, only now we knew they were moving and sensing the air and our departure. We knew they continued like that all night while we slept.

Halfway back to the house, the building we moved towards seemed to be stuffed with something yellow and wet. The night, the dark air, made it all mad. That 15 yards away there were bright birds in cages and here John Chisum and I walked in our strange bodies. Around us total blackness, nothing out there but a desert for 70 miles or more, and to the left, a few yards away, a house stuffed with wet light where within the frame of a window we saw a woman move carrying fire in a glass funnel and container towards the window, towards the edge of the dark where we stood.

*

The street of slow-moving animals
while the sun drops in perfect verticals
no wider than boots
The dogs sleep their dreams off
they are everywhere
so that horses on the crowded weekend
will step back and snap a leg

while I've been going on
blood from my wrist
has travelled to my heart
and my fingers touch
this soft blue paper notebook
control a pencil that shifts up and sideways
mapping my thinking going its own way
like light wet glasses drifting on polished wood.

The acute nerves spark
on the periphery of our bodies
while the block trunk of us
blunders as if we were
those sun-drugged horses

I am here with the range for everything
corpuscle muscle hair
hands that need the rub of metal
those senses that
want to crash things with an axe
that listen to deep buried veins in our palms

those who move in dreams over women, night
near you, every paw, the invisible hooves
the mind's invisible blackout   the intricate never
the body's waiting rut.

*

She leans against the door, holds
her left hand at the elbow
with her right, looks at the bed

on my sheets—oranges
peeled half-peeled
bright as hidden coins against the pillow

she walks slow to the window
lifts the sackcloth
and jams it horizontal on a nail
so the bent oblong of sun
hoists itself across the room
framing the bed the white flesh
of my arm

she is crossing the sun
sits on her leg here
sweeping off the peels

traces the thin bones on me
turns toppling slow back to the pillow
Bonney Bonney

I am very still
I take in all the angles of the room

*

This nightmare by a 7-foot-high doorway
waiting for friends to come
mine or theirs
I am inside the room
in the brown cold dark
the doorway's slide of sun
3 inches from my shoes
I am on the edge of the cold dark
watching the white landscape in its frame
a world that's so precise
every nail and cobweb
has magnified itself to my presence

Waiting
nothing breaks my vision
but flies in their black path
like inverted stars,
or the shock sweep of a bird
that's grown too hot
and moves into the cool for an hour

If I hold up my finger
I blot out the horizon
if I hold up my thumb
I'd ignore a man who comes
on a 3-mile trip to here
The dog near me breathes out
his lungs make a pattern of sound
when he shakes
his ears go off like whips

he is outside the door, his mind
clean, the heat
floating his brain in fantasy

I am here on the edge of sun
that would ignite me
looking out into pitch-white
sky and grass overdeveloped to meaninglessness
waiting for enemies' friends or mine

There is nothing in my hands
though every move I would make
getting up slowly walking
on the periphery of black
to where weapons are
is planned by my eye

A boy blocks out the light
in blue shirt and jeans
his long hair over his ears
face young like some pharaoh

I am unable to move
with nothing in my hands

*

Patrick Garrett had stuffed birds. Not just the stringy Mexican vultures but huge exotic things. We would sometimes be with him when they arrived. He would have them sent to him frozen in boxes. The box was wooden, a crate really, and with great care after bringing it back from the station, he would remove the nails. He took out the 8″ of small crushed ice and said look. And it would be a white seagull, beautifully spread in the ice, not a feather out of place, its claws extended, and brittle from the freezing. Garrett melted it and split it with a narrow knife, parting the feathers first, and with a rubber glove in his right hand removed the body. He washed the rotted blood from the wings, the outside, and then took it out onto the verandah to dry.

*

The end of it, lying at the wall
the bullet itch frozen in my head

my right arm is through the glass pane
and the cut veins awake me
so I can watch inside and through the window

Garrett's voice going Billy Billy
and the other two dancing circles
saying we got him we got him the little shrunk bugger

the pain at my armpit I'm glad for
keeping me alive at the bone
and suns coming up everywhere out of the walls and floors
Garrett's jaw and stomach   thousands

of lovely perfect sun balls
breaking at each other click
click click click like Saturday morning pistol cleaning
when the bullets hop across the bedsheet and bounce and click

click and you toss them across the floor like . . . up in the air
and see how many you can catch in one hand the left

oranges reeling across the room and I KNOW I KNOW
it is my brain coming out like red grass
this breaking where red things wade

Burning Hills

So he came to write again
in the burnt hill region
north of Kingston. A cabin
with mildew spreading down walls.
Bullfrogs on either side of him.

Hanging his lantern of Shell Vapona Strip
on a hook in the centre of the room
he waited a long time. Opened
the Hilroy writing pad, yellow Bic pen.
Every summer he believed would be his last.
This schizophrenic season change, June to September,
when he deviously thought out plots
across the character of his friends.
Sometimes barren as fear going nowhere
or in habit meaningless as tap water.
One year maybe he would come and sit
for four months and not write a word down
would sit and investigate colours, the
insects in the room with him.

What he brought: a typewriter
cans of ginger ale, cigarettes. A copy of *Strangelove,*
of *The Intervals,* a postcard of Rousseau's *The Dream.*
His friends' words were strict as lightning
unclothing the bark of a tree, a shaved hook.
The postcard was a test pattern by the window
through which he saw growing scenery.

Eventually the room was a time machine for him.
He closed the rotting door, sat down

thought pieces of history. The first girl
who in a park near his school
put a warm hand into his trousers
unbuttoning and finally catching the spill
across her wrist, he in the maze of her skirt.
She later played the piano
when he had tea with the parents.
He remembered that surprised—
he had forgotten for so long.
Under raincoats in the park on hot days.

The summers were layers of civilization in his memory
they were old photographs he didn't look at anymore
for girls in them were not as perfect as in his mind
and his ungovernable hair was shaved to the edge of skin.
His friends leaned on bicycles
were 16 and tried to look 21
the cigarettes too big for their faces.
He could read those characters easily,
undisguised as wedding pictures.
He could hardly remember their names
though they had talked all day, exchanged styles
and like dogs on a lawn hung around the houses of girls,
singing dramatically in someone's ear along with the record
'How do you think I feel / you know our love's not real.'
He saw all that complex tension the way his children would.

There is one picture that fuses the five summers.
Eight of them are leaning against a wall
arms around each other
looking into the camera and the sun
trying to smile at the unseen adult photographer
trying against the glare to look 21 and confident.
That summer and friendship will last forever.

Except one who was eating an apple. That was him
oblivious to the significance of the moment.
Now he hungers to have that arm around the next shoulder.
The wretched apple is fresh and white.

Since he began burning hills
the Shell strip has taken effect.
A wasp is crawling on the floor
tumbling over, its motor fanatic.
He has smoked 5 cigarettes.
He has written slowly and carefully
with great love and great coldness.
When he finishes he will go back
hunting for the lies that are obvious.

Claude Glass

> A somewhat convex dark or coloured hand-mirror, used to concentrate the features of the landscape in subdued tones.

> *'Gray walked about everywhere with that pretty toy, the Claude Lorraine glass, in his hand, making the beautiful forms of the landscape compose in its lustrous chiaroscuro.'* —EDMUND GOSSE

He is told about
the previous evening's behaviour.
Starting with a punchbowl
on the volleyball court
dancing and falling across coffee tables,
asking his son Are *you* the bastard
who keeps telling me I'm drunk?
kissing the limbs of women
suspicious of his friends serenading
five pigs by the barn
heaving a wine glass towards a garden
and continually going through gates
into the dark fields and collapsing.
                                        And even later
his thirteen-year-old daughter's struggle
to lift him into the back kitchen
after he passed out, resting his head on rocks,
wondering what he was looking for in dark fields.

For he has always loved that ancient darkness
where flat rocks glide like Japanese tables
where he can remove clothes
and lie with moonlight on the day's heat
hardened in stone, drowning
under this star blanket of sky

conscious how the heavens
careen over him
as he moves in fields
kissing the limbs of trees
and then turns to watch the house
in its oasis of light.
And he knows something is happening there to him
solitary while he spreads his arms
and holds everything that is slipping away together.

He is suddenly in the heat of the party
revolving round one unhappy shadow.
That friend who said he would find
the darkest place, and then wave.
He is not a lost drunk
like his father or his friend, can,
he says, stop on a dime, and he can
he could because even now, in
this brilliant darkness where
grass has lost its colour and it's all
fucking Yeats and moonlight, he knows
this colourless grass is making his bare feet green
for it is the hour of magic
which no matter what sadness
leaves him grinning.
At certain hours of the night
ducks are nothing but landscape
just voices breaking as they nightmare.
The weasel wears their blood
home like a scarf,
cows drain over the horizon
                                        and the dark
vegetables hum underground
but the mouth
            wants plum.

Moves from room to room
where beer glass
smashed lounges at his feet
opens the long rust-stained gate
and steps towards invisible fields
that he knows from years of daylight.
By the kitchen sink he tells someone
From now on I will drink only landscapes
—here, pour me a cup of Spain.

Opens the gate again and stumbles
away from the lights, unbuttoning,
recalls his drunk invitation to the river
steering the car past sugarbush
to the blue night water,
and steps out speaking to branches,
the subtle applause of animals.

He falls back onto the intricacies
of gearshift and steering wheel
alive as his left arm which
now departs out of the window
trying to tug passing sumac,
pine, tamarack into
the car,
                to the party.

On the front lawn a sheet, tacked
across a horizontal branch.
A projector starts a parade of journeys,
landscapes, relatives, friends
leaping out within pebbles of water
caught by the machine as if creating rain.

Later when wind frees the sheet
and it collapses like powder in the grass
pictures fly without target
and howl their colours over Southern Ontario
clothing burdock
rhubarb a floating duck.
Landscapes and stories
flung into branches
and the dog walks under the hover of the swing
beam of the projection bursting in his left eye.
Someone gets up and heaves his glass
into the vegetable patch
towards the slow stupid career of beans.

This is the hour
when dead men sit
and write each other.

> 'Concerning the words we never said
> during morning hours of the party
> there was glass under my bare feet
> laws of the kitchen were broken
> and each word moved
> in my mouth like muscle . . .'

This is the hour for sudden journeying,
when Cervantes accepts an invitation
from the Chinese emperor.
Schools of Chinese–Spanish linguistics!
Rivers of the world meet!

At 4 a.m. he wakes in the sheet
that earlier held tropics in its whiteness.
The invited river flows through the house

into the kitchen, upstairs,
he awakens and moves within it.
In the dim light he sees
the Turkish carpet underwater,
low stools, glint of piano pedals,
even a sleeping dog
whose dreams may be of rain.

It is a river he has walked elsewhere
now visiting moving with him at the hip
to the kitchen where a friend sleeps in a chair
head on the table his grip
still round a glass, legs underwater.

He wants to relax
and give in to the night
fall horizontal and swim
to the back kitchen where his daughter sleeps.
He wishes to travel
to each of his family and gaze
at their underwater dreaming
this magic chain of bubbles,
the household guests, all
comfortable in clean river water.

He is aware that for hours
there has been no conversation,
tongues have slid to stupidity on alcohol
sleeping mouths are photographs of yells.

He stands waiting, a sentinel,
shambling back and forth, his anger
and desire against the dark

which, if he closes his eyes,
will lose them all.

The oven light
shines up through water at him
a bathysphere a ghost ship
and in the half-drowned room
crickets like small pins
begin to tack down
the black canvas of this night,
begin to talk their hesitant
gnarled epigrams to each other
across the room.
Creak and echo.
Creak and echo. With absolute clarity
he knows where he is.

TIN ROOF

'She hesitated. "Are you being romantic now?"
"I'm trying to tell you how I feel without
exposing myself. You know what I mean?"'

—ELMORE LEONARD

*

You stand still for three days
for a piece of wisdom
and everything falls to the right place

or wrong place

and look through windows
for cue cards
blazing in the sky.

The solution.

This last year I was sure
I was going to die

*

The geography of this room   I know so well
tonight, I could rise in the dark
sit at the table   and write without light.
I am here in the country of warm rains.
A small cabin—a glass, wood,
tin bucket on the Pacific Rim.

Geckoes climb the window to peer in,
and all day the tirade pale blue waves
touch the black shore of volcanic rock

and fall to pieces here

*

How to arrive at this
drowning
on the edge of sea

(How to drive
the Hana road, he said—
one hand on the beer
one hand on your thigh
and one eye for the road)

Waves leap to this cliff all day
and in the evening lose
their pale blue

he rises from the bed
as wind from three directions
falls, takes his place
on the peninsula of sheets
which also loses colour

stands by a window and gazes

through gecko
past the deadfall
into sea,
the blue heart

*

Rainy night talk

Here's to
the woman from Kansas
whispering good morning at five,
dazed
in balcony moonlight

All that drizzle the night before
walking through rain

Here's to her driving home that night
in more and more rain
weaving like a one-sided
lonely conversation
over the mountains

And what were you
carrying? in your head
that night Miss
Souri? Miss Kansas?

while I put my hands
sweating
on the cold
window
on the edge
of the trough of this city?

*

Tell me
all you know
about bamboo

growing wild, green
growing up into soft arches
in the temple ground

the traditions

driven through hands
through the heart
during torture

and most of all

this

small bamboo pipe
not quite horizontal
that drips
every ten seconds
to a shallow bowl

I love this
being here
not a word
just the faint
fall of liquid
the boom of an iron Buddhist bell
in the heart rapid
as ceremonial bamboo

*

The cabin
                its tin roof
a wind-run radio
catches the noise of the world.
He focuses on the gecko
its almost transparent body
how he feels now
everything passing through him like light.
In certain mirrors
he cannot see himself at all.
He is joyous and breaking down.
The tug over the cliff.
What protects him
is the warmth in the sleeve

that is all, really

*

A man buying wine
Rainier beer at the store
would he be satisfied with this?
Cold showers, electric skillet,
Red River on tv
Oh he could be

(Do you want
                    to be happy and write?)

He happens to love the starkness
of this place, the refusal
to move

All our narratives a mild rumble
to those inland

His heart like a sleeve

*

2 a.m.   in the kitchen

I want

the woman whose face
I could not believe in the moonlight
her mouth forever as horizon

and both of us
grim with situation

*

You say, this
doesn't happen so quick
I must remind you of someone

No,
though I am seduced
by this light, and
frantic arguments
on the porch,
I ain't subtle
you run rings
round me

but now our quietness

the white dress   long legs
arguing your body
away from me

and I with all the hunger
I didn't know I had

*

cabin
this *flower* of wood
in which we rose
out of the blue sheets
reaching for lamp or book
my shirt

hungry
for everything about the other

here we steal places to stay
as we steal time
never too proud to beg,
even if we never
see the other's grin and star again

there is nothing resigned
in this briefness
we swallow complete

I will know everything here

this cup
balanced on my chest
my eye witnessing the petal
drop away from its order,
your arm

for ever

precarious in all our fury

*

We go to the stark places of the earth
and find moral questions everywhere

Tonight I lean over the Pacific
and its blue wild silk
ringed by creatures
who
    tchick tchick tchick
my sudden movement
who say nothing else.

There are those who are in
and those who look in

Tiny leather toes
hug the glass

*

Every place has its own wisdom. Come,
time we talked about the sea,
the long waves
                    trapped around islands

*

On the porch
thin ceramic
chimes

        ride wind
off the Pacific

bells of the sea

        I do not know
the name of large orange flowers
which thrive on salt air
lean half drunk
against the steps

Untidy banana trees
thick moss on the cliff
and then the plunge
to black volcanic shore

It is impossible to enter the sea here
except in a violent way

        How we have moved
from thin ceramic

to such destruction

*

All night

                    the touch

of wave on volcano.

There was the woman
who clutched my hair
like a shaken child.
The radio whistles
round a lost wavelength.

All night slack-key music
and the bird whistling *duino*
duino, words and music
entangled in pebble
ocean static.
The wild sea and her civilization
the League of the Divine Wind
and traditions of death.

                        Remember
those women in movies
who wept into the hair
of their dead men?

*

Going up stairs
I hang my shirt
on the stiff
ear of an antelope

Above the bed
        memory
restless bamboo
        the distant army
assembles wooden spears

her feet braced
on the ceiling
sea in the eye

Reading the article
an 1825 report *Physiologie du goût.*
on the artificial growing of truffles
speaks
of 'vain efforts!'
and 'deceitful promises!'
commandments of culinary art

Good
morning to your body
and appendix scar like a letter
of too much passion
from a mad Mexican doctor

All this noise at your neck!
heart clapping like green bamboo

this earring
that has flipped over
    and fallen
        into the pool of your ear

The waves against black stone
that was a thousand-year-old
burning red river
could not reach us

*

There are maps now whose portraits
have nothing to do with surface

Remember the angels, floating compasses
—portolan atlases so complex
we looked down and never knew
which was earth which was sea.
The way birds the colour of prairie
confused by sky
flew into the earth
(Remember those women
who claimed dead miners
the colour of the coal they drowned in)

The bathymetric maps startle.
Visions of the ocean floor
troughs, naked blue deserts,
Ganges Cone, the Mascarene Basin

so one is able now
in ideal situations
to plot a stroll
to new continents
doing 'the Berryman walk'

And beneath the sea
these giant scratches
of pain
the markings of
some perfect animal
who has descended

burying itself
under the glossy
ballroom

or they have to do with ascending,
what we were, the earth creatures
longing for horizon.
I know one thing
our sure non-sliding
civilized feet
our small leather shoes
did not make them

(Ah you should be happy and write)

I want the passion
which puts your feet on the ceiling

takes us
          somehow
out of the rooms of poetry

(Listen, solitude, someone said,
is not an absolute,
just a resting place)

and in the end the pivot
depends on small things
the question
are you happy?

No I am not happy

lucky though

*

Breaking down after logical rules
Couldn't be the hit-and-run driver

Could write my suite of poems
of Bogart, drunk, after the departure at Casablanca,
or lying below a fan
at the Slavianski Bazaar Hotel
seeing only truth in the space
between the whirling metal

knocks the bottle
leaning against his bare stomach
onto the sheet. Gin stems
out like a four-leaf clover.
                                        And that
was a movie I saw just once.

What about Burt Lancaster
limping away at the end of *Trapeze*?
(I grew up knowing I could never fly)

That's me. You. Educated
at the Bijou. And don't ask me
about my interpretation of 'Madame George.'
That's a nine-minute song
a two-hour story

So how do we discuss
the education of our children?
Teach them to be romantics

to veer towards the sentimental?
Toss them into the air
and make them do the triple somersault
through all these complexities
and commandments?

*

Oh, Rilke, I want to sit down calm like you
or pace the castle, avoiding the path of the cook, Carlo,
who believes down to his turnip soup
that you speak in the voice of the devil.
I want the long lines my friend spoke of
that bamboo which sways muttering
like wooden teeth in the slim volume I have
with its childlike drawing of Duino Castle.
I have circled your book for years
like a wave combing
the green hair of the sea,
kept it with me. Your name
a password in the alley.
I always wanted poetry to be that
but this solitude brings no wisdom
just two-day-old food in the fridge,
certain habits you would not approve of.
If I said all of your name now
it would be the movement
of the tide you soared over
so your private angel
could become part of a map.

I am too often busy with things
I wish to get away from, and I want
the line to move slowly now, slow
-ly like a careful drunk across the street
no cars in the vicinity
but in his fearful imagination.
How can I link your flowing name
to geckoes or a slice of octopus?

Though there are Rainier beer cans,
magically, on the windowsill.

And still your lovely letters
January 1912 near Trieste.
The car you were driven in
'at a snail's pace'
through Provence. Wanting
'to go into chrysalis . . .
to live by the heart and nothing else.'

So at midnight we remember the colour
of a dogwood flower outside the window.

I wanted poetry to be walnuts
in their green cases
but now it is the sea
and we let it drown us,
and we fly to it released
by giant catapults
of pain loneliness deceit and vanity

ROCK BOTTOM

TWO PHOTOGRAPHS

It was years earlier, you in an old bathtub
with barely a few inches of water,
on an island, the weather outside unknown
but for the tan that surrounded your whiteness

Everything suggested an era long before the present,
the late sixties perhaps, a weekday afternoon
with little to show how you spent your days, your nights

Just two black-and-white photographs.
The first capturing your gaze into nowhere
the other when you covered your face with your hands
so you were not anonymous, only unseen
except perhaps by what you might be thinking

What was the year? Where was the house and town?
Nothing given away by your silence and careful movement,
'still practically a bride,' twenty years before we met

Another photograph I saw later
A more formal nude shaped by shadow
your bare feet, you in a crouch, faceless.
Not so much your image but a husband's
hovering with a camera.

Whereas everything casual in the earlier pictures
with that bathtub and that raw sunlight
makes them your ex-husband's masterpiece
—the secret of your look, the recall
of an afternoon when things will hold
or fall away

It is in these pictures, being

the unknown stranger, I hold
a complete belief in you, long before we met.

How *did* we meet I whisper even now,
as if magically that first time landing
after a far journey upon a dark
hardly lit island late at night. And then
somehow solitary with you in what
for all I know was a crowded car

*

DEPOT CREEK, ONTARIO

In a warm Ontario river
my head back

moving towards
an estuary between trees

there's a dog
learning to swim near me
friends on shore

my head dips
back to the eyebrow
I'm the prow
on an ancient vessel,
soul between my teeth

and a heron
with its awkward flap
upside down

one of us is wrong

he
in his blue-grey thud
thinking he knows
the blue way
out of here

or me

*

Came out of the water
climbed into my car and drove home
got out of the car still wet towel round me
opened the gate and walked to the house

Disintegration of the spirit
no stars
leaf being eaten by moonlight

The small creatures who are blind
who travel with the aid
of petite white horns
take over the world

Sound of a moth

The screen door in its suspicion
allows nothing in, as I allow nothing in.
The raspberries my son gave me
wild, cold out of the fridge, a few I put
in my mouth, some in my shirt pocket
and forgot

I sit here
in a half-dark kitchen
the stain at my heart
caused by this gift

*

Another deep night
with *The National Enquirer*

silence

like the unseen
arms of a bat

the book
falls open
to sadness
—dead flowers, horses
who carried
lovers to a meeting

On my last walk
through the kitchen
I see it, lift
the huge arms of a cobweb
out of the air
and carry its Y
slowly to the porch
as if alive

as if a wounded bird
or some camouflaged insect
that could damage children

*

The three trunks
of the walnut tree

ceremonial ducks
who limbo under the fence
and creep up the lawn

An apple tree   a blue-and-white house
I know this is beautiful

I wished to write today
about small things
that might persuade me
out of my want

The lines I read
about 'cowardice' and 'loyalty'
I don't know
if this is drowning
or coming up for air

*

The distance between us
and then this small map
of stars
            a concentrated
ocean of the night

when lovers worship heavens
they are worshipping
a lack of distance

my brother the moon
the lofty mattress
of nebula,
rash and spray of love

                  It is all
as close as my palm
on your body
                              so you
among pillows and moonlight
look up, search
for my dark hand

*

After Che-King, 11th Century BC:
'If you love me and think only of me
lift your robe and ford the river Chen'

catch
            the floating world
8:52 from Chicago

lift your skirt
through customs,

kiss me in the parking lot

*

What were the names of the towns
we drove into and through

stunned   lost

having drunk our way
up vineyards
and then hot springs
boiling out the drunkenness

What were the names
I slept through
my head
on your thigh
hundreds of miles
of blackness entering the car

All this
darkness and stars
but now
under the Napa Valley night
a star arch of dashboard
the ripe grape moon
we are together
and I love this muscle

I love this muscle
that tenses

and joins
the accelerator
to my cheek

*

THE DESIRE UNDER THE ELMS MOTEL

How I attempted seduction
with a select and
careful playing of
the McGarrigle Sisters

how you seduced me
stereophonically   the laugh

the nose   ankle   nature

        repartee   the knee

your sad determination   letters

the earring

            that falls

            'hey love—

            you forgot your glove'

*

In a Toronto tavern
3 p.m. the only one busy
is the waitress
who reads a book a day

Hour of the afternoon soaps
Men bursting into bedrooms
out of restaurants,
talking on phones
to the lover's brother
or the husband's mistress

The pastel bar
grey colours of the tv
this is where people come
after the second failure of redemption

*

'A FRIED EGG SANDWICH AT 1 A.M.'

Midnight dinner at the Vesta Lunch
Here there is nothing
I have taken from you
so I begin with memory
as old songs do

                    in this café
against the night

in this villa refrain
where we collect the fragments
no longer near us
to make ourselves whole

                    your bright eyes
in a Greek bar, the way
you wear your hat

*

GOODBYE

I write about you
as if I own you
which I do not.
As you can say of nothing
this is mine.

When we rise
the last hug
no longer belongs,
is your fiction
or my story.

Whether we pass
through each other
like pure arrows
or fade into rumour
I write down now
a fiction of your arm

or of that afternoon
in Union Station
when we both were lost
pain falling free
the speed of tears
under the Grand Rotunda
as we disappeared
rose from each other

you and your arrow
taking just
what you fled through

*

Speaking to you
these days when
I have lost the feather of poetry
and the rains
of separation
surround us

Everyone has learned
to move carefully

'Dancing' 'laughing' 'bad taste'
is a memory
a tableau behind trees of law

In the midst of love for you
my wife's suffering
anger in every direction
and the children wise
as tough shrubs
but they are not tough
—so I fear
how anything can grow from this

all the wise blood
poured from little cuts
down into the sink

this hour it is not
your body I want
but your quiet company

*

Dentists disguise their own bad teeth
barbers go bald, foolish birds
travel to one particular tree.
They pride themselves
on focus.
Poets cannot spell.
Everyone claims abstinence.

Reading Neruda to a class
reading his lovely old
curiosity about all things
I am told this is the first time
in months I seem happy.
Jealous of his slide
through complexity.
All afternoon I keep
stepping into his pocket

                    whispering
instruct and delight me

*

THESE BACK ALLEYS

for Daphne, 1974

In '64 you moved
and where was I?
—somewhere and married
(In '64 everybody got married)

Whatever we are now we were then,
though some maps collide, fall into the future

It seems for hours
we have sat in your car,
almost Valentine's Day

I've got a plane to meet and I
hold your rose for you.
This talk between us
like a slow dance,
the sharing of earphones

Since I've been separated
I cannot hold my brain
in my hands anymore.
We watch each other
in our slow walks into
and out of everything
we wanted to know in '64

While for George 'moonlight
became her.' Curious, after years of wit
he saw it enter her and believed,
singing love songs in the back scat

So the three of us drive downtown
in our confusions.
Goodbye to the hills of our thirties

George still 'hearty,' his bad jokes
scattering to the group,
does not converse,
                    but he sings the heartbreakers
badly but precisely in the back seat

so we moon, we tough

*

For you I have slept
like an arrow in the hall
pointing towards your wakefulness
in other time zones

while
piece by piece
we put ourselves together
your past that of one
who has walked through
fifteen strange houses
in order to be here

the charm of 19th-century Wichita
in your bones—
that history
I read in books and on the flickering screen
when I was thirteen

. . . now that child
still hugs against her
Goodnight Moon

reading its courtly order,
its list of farewells from
prairie to tropics

strange how, however briefly

history
focuses

*

Kissing the stomach
kissing your scarred
skin boat. History
is what you've travelled on
and take with you

We've each had our stomachs
kissed by strangers
to the other

and as for me
I bless everyone
who kissed you here

SKIN BOAT

The Then

A strange awakening thought at 7 a.m.

to erase this life, and desire what I might have known
in photographs of you before we met

where I could have circled you
at a tactful distance, being told only
about your husband

but nothing of the rules you owned
about yourself, how you raised your children,
were in constant argument with Kailua city planners

Or even before, during that slow crawl
of tectonic plates across the Pacific
into the future with us unaware
of each other at some high-school dance,
a drunken party, or the boy
who was invited to your heartbeat
under a kimono

The *then*.

All that history until we met
in furious chaos when I loved first
your face, then loved how you
had become what you were

How long did all those possibilities sleep
during the years
before this emerging?

The Cinnamon Peeler

If I were a cinnamon peeler
I would ride your bed
and leave the yellow bark dust
on your pillow.

Your breasts and shoulders would reek
you could never walk through markets
without the profession of my fingers
floating over you. The blind would
stumble certain of whom they approached
though you might bathe
under rain gutters, monsoon.

Here on the upper thigh
at this smooth pasture
neighbour to your hair
or the crease
that cuts your back. This ankle.
You will be known among strangers
as the cinnamon peeler's wife.

I could hardly glance at you
before marriage
never touch you
—your keen nosed mother,
your rough brothers.
I buried my hands
in saffron, disguised them
over smoking tar,
helped the honey gatherers . . .

When we swam once
I touched you in water
and our bodies remained free,
you could hold me and be blind of smell.
You climbed the bank and said

this is how you touch other women
the grass cutter's wife, the lime burner's daughter.
And you searched your arms
for the missing perfume

and knew

what good is it
to be the lime burner's daughter
left with no trace
as if not spoken to in the act of love
as if wounded without the pleasure of a scar.

You touched
your belly to my hands
in the dry air and said
I am the cinnamon
peeler's wife. Smell me.

Women Like You

The communal poem—Sigiri Graffiti, 6th century

They do not stir
these ladies of the mountain
do not give us
the twitch of eyelids
answer no one
take only the hard rock as lover

Women like you
make men pour out their hearts

who came here out of the bleached land
climbed this fortress
to adore the rock
and with the solitude of the air
behind them
                carved an alphabet
whose motive was perfect desire

wanting these portraits of women
to speak and caress,
so hundreds of small verses
by different hands
became one
habit of the unrequited

Seeing you
I want no other life

Everywhere below is jungle, waves of heat
secular love

A circle of first finger
and thumb
              a window
to your breast
pleasure of the skin
curl of the belly
                    and then
a stone heart

We stand against the sky

I bring you
a flute
from the throat
of a loon

So talk to me
of the used heart

The River Neighbour

All these rumours. You lodge in the mountains
of Hang-chou, a cabin in Portland township,
or in Yüeh-chou for sure

the dust from my marriage
wasted our clear autumn

while you lounge with my children
by creek snakes, field asparagus

Across the universe
each room I lit
was a dark garden, I held
nothing but the lamp

(This letter paints me
transparent as I am)

I find her earrings
at the foot of curtainless windows
In the kitchen
salt fills the body
of an RCA Victor dog

Let us nose our way
next year with the spring waters
and search for each other
somewhere in the east

To a Sad Daughter

All night long the hockey pictures
gaze down at you
sleeping in your tracksuit.
Belligerent goalies are your ideal.
Threats of being traded
cuts and wounds
—all this pleases you.
O my god! you say at breakfast
reading the sports page over the Alpen
as another player breaks his ankle
or assaults the coach.

When I thought of daughters
I wasn't expecting this
but I like this more.
I like all your faults
even your purple moods
when you retreat from everyone
to sit in bed under a quilt.
And when I say 'like'
I mean of course 'love'
but that embarrasses you.
You who feel superior to black-and-white movies
(coaxed for hours to see *Casablanca*)
though you were moved
by *Creature from the Black Lagoon.*

One day I'll come swimming
beside your ship or someone will
and if you hear the siren
listen to it. For if you close your ears
only nothing happens. You will never change.

I don't care if you risk
your life to angry goalies
creatures with webbed feet.
You can enter their caves and castles
their glass laboratories. Just
don't be fooled by anyone but yourself.

This is the first lecture I've given you.
You're 'sweet sixteen' you said.
I'd rather be your closest friend
than your father. I'm not good at advice
you know that, but ride
the ceremonies
until they grow dark.

Sometimes you are so busy
discovering your friends
I ache with a loss
—but that is greed.
And sometimes I've gone
into *my* purple world
and lost you.

One afternoon I stepped
into your room. You were sitting
at the desk where I now write this.
Forsythia outside the window
and sun spilled over you
like a thick yellow miracle
as if another planet
was coaxing you out of the house
—all those possible worlds!—
and you, meanwhile, busy with mathematics.

I cannot look at forsythia now
without loss, or joy for you.
You step delicately
into the wild world
and your real prize will be
the frantic search.
Want everything. If you break
break going out not in.
How you live your life I don't care
but I'll sell my arms for you,
hold your secrets forever.

If I speak of death
which you fear now, greatly,
it is without answers,
except that each
one we know is
in our blood.
Don't recall graves.
Memory is permanent.
Remember the afternoon's
yellow suburban annunciation.
Your goalie
in his frightening mask
dreams perhaps
of gentleness.

All Along the Mazinaw

Later the osprey
falling towards
only what he sees

the messenger heron
warning of our progress
up Mud Lake

a paddle is stranger
to what it heaves out of the way

Wherever you go
within a silence
is witnessed,

everything aware
of alteration but you,
creatures who veer,
a torn leaf descending

In rapids
rocks gaze up
with the bright paint
of previous canoes

But now only you, for an hour
in the arms of the Mazinaw

those things we don't know we love
we love harder

Pacific Letter

to Stan of Depot Creek, old friend, pal o'mine

Now I remember that you rebuilt my chicken coop
north of the farmhouse along the pasture fence
with fresh pine from Verona.
In autumn you hid a secret message under floorboards
knowing we would find it in spring.
A fanciful message. Carved with care.
As you carved you imagined the laughing.
We both know the pleasures art and making bring.

And in summer we lounged for month on month
letting slide the publishers and English Departments
who sent concerned letters that slept in the red mailbox.
Men and women came drifting in
from the sea and from the west border
and with them there was nothing at cross purposes.
They made nothing of mountain crossing
to share that fellowship.
The girls danced because
their long sleeves would not keep still
and I, drunk, went to sleep among field rocks.
We spoke our desires without regret.
Then you returned to the west of the province
and I to the south.

After separation had come to its worst
we met and travelled the Mazinaw with our sons
through all the thirty-six folds of that creature river
into the valley of bright lichen,
green rice beds, marble rock, and at night
slept under croaking pine.
The spirit so high it was all over the heavens!

And at Depot Creek we walked
for a last time downriver
to a neighbour's southern boundary
past the tent where you composed verses
past the land where I once lived
the water about it clear in my memory as jade.
Then you and your wife sang back and forth
in the mosquito-filled cabin under the naphtha.
The muskrat, listening at the edge,
heard our sound—guitars and lone violin
whose weavings seduced us with sadness.

The canoe brushed over open lake
hearing the lit homes
whose laughter eliminated the paddle
and a loon stumbled into the air
shocked us awake and disappeared,
slid the moon away,
and before the last days in August
we scattered like stars and rain.

And I think now that this
is what we are to each other,
friends busy with their own distance
who reappear now and then.
As once you could not believe
I had visited the town of your youth
where you sat in your room
perfecting 'Heartbreak Hotel'
that new place to dwell—that
tender word in the midst of angry song.

All this comes to an end.
During summer evenings

I miss your company.
Things we clung to
remain on the horizon
so we become the loon
on his journey
to confused depth and privacy.

At such times—no talking
no conclusion in the heart.

I buy postage
                seal this

and send it a thousand miles, thinking.

Translations of My Postcards

the peacock means order
fighting kangaroos mean madness
an oasis means I have struck water

positioning of the stamp—the despot's head
horizontal, or mounted policemen,
mean political danger

the false date means I
am not where I should be

when I speak of the weather
I mean business

a blank postcard says
I am in the wilderness

A Dog in Berkeley

Sitting in an empty house
with a dog from the Mexican circus!
O Daisy, embrace is my only pleasure.
Holding and hugging my friends. Education.
A wave of eucalyptus. Warm granite.
These are the things I have in my heart.
Heart and skills, there's nothing else.

I usually don't like small dogs but you
like midwestern women take over the air.
You leap into the air and pivot
a diver going up! You are known
to open the fridge and eat when you wish
you can roll down car windows and step out
you know when to get off the elevator.

I always wanted to be a dog
but I hesitated
for I thought they lacked certain skills.
Now I want to be a dog.

Her House

Because she has lived alone, her house is the product of nothing but herself and necessity. The necessity of growing older and raising children. Others drifted into her life, in and out and they have changed her, added things, but I have never been into a home that is a revelation of character and time as much as hers. It contains those she knows and has known. When I first met her I saw nothing but her, and now, as she becomes familiar, I recognize the small customs.

The problem for her is leaving. She says, 'Last night I was listening to everything I know so well, and I imagined what if I woke up in a year's time and there were different trees.' Streets, the weight of sea air, certain birds who recognize your shrubbery, that too holds you, allows a freedom of habit, is a house.

Everything here is alien to me but you. Your room like a grey well, your coat hangers above the laundry machine where you hang the semi-damp clothes, so you do not have to iron them, the green-grey walls of wood, the secret drawer which you opened after you knew me two years to show me the ancient Japanese pens. All this I love. Though I carry my own landscape in me. But this has become your skin, and as you leave you recognize this.

On certain evenings, when I have not bothered to put on lights, I hit my knees on low bookcases where they should not be. But you shift your hip easily, habitually, around them as you pass by carrying laundry or books. When you can move through a house blindfolded it belongs to you, moving like blood calmly within your own body. It is only recently

I am able to wake beside you and without looking, almost in a dream, put out my hand and know exactly where your shoulder or your heart will be—you in your specific posture in this bed of yours that we share. And at times this has seemed to be knowledge. As if you are a blueprint of your house.

Bessie Smith at Roy Thomson Hall

At first she refused to sing.

She had applied for the one concert—that she was allowed each sabbatical—to take place in Havana. Palms! Oh pink walls! Cuba! she would hum to herself, dazzling within the clouds.

But here she was. Given the choice of nine Honest Ed restaurants and then hurried to Roy Thomson Hall which certainly should never have been called that.

A long brown dress, with fringes. Fred Longshaw at the piano.

She opened the first set with 'Kitchen Man.' Five people left. Al Neil had flown in from Vancouver on a tip. For the next ten minutes, after people realized it really *was* Bessie Smith, the hall was filled with shouted requests. 'Any Woman's Blues,' 'Down in the Dumps' . . . until she said I want to sing what I never was allowed to, because I died. And she brought the rest of the twentieth century under her wing.

She wore wings. They raised themselves with her arms each time she coaxed a phrase. Her wings would float up and fall slow like a hand held out of a car coming down against the wind, the feathers black as the Steinway. You should have been there.

During the intermission the stunned audience just sat in their seats. 'She's looking good' was one of the common remarks.

Then she returned and brought out the band. They were glad to have arrived on earth, but they too had hoped for Havana. Abraham Wheat on soprano sax was there. Joe Smith on cornet was there. By midnight her voice was even better. She talked more between songs.

At 2 a.m. the band levitated. She used no microphone. Above us banners waved and danced like a multitude. She took on and caressed the songs of Jerome Kern. She asked what happened to her friend Charlie Green. And then, to her surprise, to apologize for Toronto, Charlie Green was allowed to join her. He had been found frozen in a Harlem tenement but now stepped forward shyly with his trombone. And he and Joe Smith and Bessie Smith were alone onstage the audience quiet and the banners still and the air-conditioning holding its breath. They wheeled away the Steinway. They brought out an old upright decorated with bullet holes, and Al Neil was asked to sit in. She sang, 'It Won't Be You.' Her encore was made up of two songs: 'Weeping Willow Blues' and 'Far Away Blues.'

We stood like sudden wheat. But she could not hear us. She could not see us. Then she died again.

Red Accordion—An Immigrant Song

How you and I talked!
Casually, and side by side,
not even cold at 4 a.m.
New Year's morning,
in a double outhouse in Blyth, Ontario.

The creak of trees and scrub snow.

Was it dream or true memory this
casualness, this ease of talk
after the long night of the previous year.
Nothing important said
just as now the poem
draws together frail times,
steps forward as accident.

                                        So we sit
within loose walls of a poem
you and I, our friends indoors
drunk on homemade wine.
All of us searching to discern
the gift we can give each other,
to speak of this landscape
or the one we came from.

And this is magic, like Ray Bird's wine
                —transformed! Finally made good.
Just as over the years,
the intricate knowledge
now of each other makes love.

Ten yards away a bonfire lifts
its redness above the farmhouse
and the lean figures of children circle
to throw in branches off a Christmas tree
while the woman with long black hair
her left foot on a stump
plays a red accordion.

I step into this New Year
dancing with a small child,
Rachel, so graceful, we bowed
when the dance was over.
And the others dance
embracing, flinging
themselves away from each other.
They bow, they look up
to a full moon, a white cold sky
so even in this stilled painting
they talk a white breath at each other.

Their boots pound down the frozen earth,
children leap from and into our arms.
All of us poised and inspired by music,
friendship, and the knowledge that
each has driven for hours
over iced highways to be here bouncing
to a reel that carried itself, generations ago
north of the border, through lost towns
settled among the strange names,
and became eventually our own

all the way from Virginia.

In a Yellow Room

There was another reason for Fats Waller to record on May 8th, 1935 'I'm Gonna Sit Right Down and Write Myself a Letter.' It is for this moment, driving from Goderich towards and past Blyth, avoiding Blyth by taking the gravel concessions, four adults and a child, who have just swum in a very cold Lake Huron. His piano drips from the cassette player and we all recognize the piece but are mute. We cannot sing before he does, before he eases himself into the lyrics as if into a chair, this large man who is to die in 1943 sitting in a train in Kansas City, finally still.

He was always moving, grand on the street or the midnight taxi rides with Andy Razaf during which it is rumoured he wrote most of his songs. I have always loved him but I love him most in the company of friends. Because his body was a crowd and we desire to imitate such community. His voice staggers or is gentle behind a whimsical piano, the melody ornamental and cool as vichyssoise in that hot studio in this hot car on a late June Ontario summer day. What else of great importance happened on May 8th, 1935?

The only creature I've ever met who disliked him was a nervous foxhound I had for three years. As soon as I put on Mr Waller the dog would dart from the room and hide under a bed. The dog recognized the anarchy, the unfolding of musical order, the growls and muttering, the fact that Fats Waller was talking to someone over your shoulder as well as to you. What my dog did not notice was the serenity he should have learned from, the notes fresh as creek-washed clothes.

The car windows open as we drive under dark maples that sniff up a rumour of the lake, with the piano energizing the hay bound into wheels, a white field of turkeys, the various tributaries of the Maitland River. Does he, drunk, and carrying his tin of tomatoes—'it feeds the body and cuts the hangover'—does he, in the midnight taxi with Razaf, imagine where the music disappears?

Where it will recur? Music and lyrics they wrote then sold to false composers for ready cash and only later admitting they had written 'On the Sunny Side of the Street' and 'I Can't Give You Anything but Love' and so many of the best songs of their time. The hidden authors on their two-hour taxi ride out of Harlem to Brooklyn and back again to Harlem, the night heat and yells overheard from the streets they passed through which they incorporated into what they were making—every texture entering this large man, a classical organist in his youth, who strode into most experiences, hid from his ex-wife Edith Hatchett, visiting two kinds of women, 'ladies who had pianos and ladies who did not,' and died of bronchial pneumonia on the Atchison, Topeka and Santa Fe, a song he did not write.

He and the great orchestra of his voice have now entered the car with us. This is his first visit to the country, though he saw it from a train window the day before he died, saw the heartland where the music could disappear, the diaspora of notes, a rewinding, a backward movement of the formation of the world, the invention of his waltz.

Breeze

for bpNichol

Nowadays I listen only to duets.
Johnny Hodges and the Bean, a thin slip
of piano behind them
on this page on this stage
craft a breeze in a horn.

One friend sits back and listens
to the other. Nowadays
I want only the wild and tender
phrasing of 'Night Hawk,'
its air groaned out
like the breath of a lover.
Rashomon by saxophone.

So brother and sister woke, miles apart,
in those 19th-century novels you loved,
with the same wound or desire.

We sit down to clean and sharpen
the other's most personal lines
—a proposal of more, a waving dismissal
of whole stanzas—in Lethbridge in Edmonton
you stood with the breeze
in an uncomfortable Chinese restaurant
in Camrose, or getting a second cup
at the Second Cup near Spadina.

I almost called you this morning
for a phone number.

Records I haven't yet returned.
Tapes you were supposed to make for me.

And across the country
tears about your death.
I always thought, someone says,
he was very good for you.
Though I still like, Barrie,
the friends who are not good for me.

Along the highway
only the duets and wind fill up my car.
I saw the scar of the jet that Sunday
trying to get you out of the sky.
Ben Webster, Coleman Hawkins.
An A and an H, a bean and a breeze.

All these twin truths

There is bright sumac, once more,
this September, along the Bayview extension

From now on
no more solos

I tie you to me

Birch Bark

for George Whalley

An hour after the storm on Birch Lake
the island bristles. Rock. Leaves still falling.
At this time, in the hour after lightning
we release the canoes.
Silence of water
purer than the silence of rock.
A paddle touches itself. We move
over blind mercury, feel the muscle
within the river, the blade
weave in dark water.

Now each casual word is precisely chosen
passed from bow to stern, as if
leaning back to pass a canteen.
There are echoes, repercussions of water.
We are in absolute landscape,
among names that fold in onto themselves.

To circle the island means witnessing
the blue-grey dust of a heron
released out of the trees.
So the dialogue slides
nothing more than friendship
an old song we break into
not needing all the words.

We are past naming the country.
The reflections are never there
without us, without the exhaustion
of water and trees after storm.

Escarpment

He lies in bed awake holding her left forearm. It is 4 a.m. He turns, his eyes rough against the night. He can hear the creek—which has no name. Yesterday at noon he walked along its shallow body overhung with cedar, beside rushes, moss, and watercress. A green-and-grey body whose intricate bones he is learning about while he stumbles and walks through in an old pair of Converse running shoes.

She was upriver investigating for herself while he explores on his own, now crawling under a tree that has uprooted and spilled its huge length across a section of the creek. He holds on to the massive stump roots and slides within the white water that heaves against him. His dreaming earlier could have involved all this.

He is looking for a wooden bridge they had crossed the previous day. He walks confidently now, the white shoes stepping casually off logs into deep water, through gravel and watercress which they will eat later in a cheese sandwich. She chews much of it walking back to the cabin. He turns and she freezes, laughing, with watercress in her mouth. There are not many more ways he can tell her he loves her. He shows mock outrage and yells but she cannot hear him over the sound of the creek.

He loves too, as she knows, the body of rivers. Provide him with a river or a creek and he will walk along it. Will step off and sink to his waist, the sound of water and rock encasing him in a solitude. Just as the noise around them insists on silence if they are more than five feet apart. It is only later when they sit in a pool legs against each other that they can talk, their conversation roaming to include relatives, books, best friends, the history of

Lewis and Clark, fragments of their past which they are piecing together. But otherwise this river's noise encases them and now he walks alone with its spirits, the clack and splash, the twig break, hearing only individual words if they occur less than an arm's length away.

He is looking, now, for a name.

It is not a name for a map—he knows the arguments of imperialism. It is a name for them, something temporary for their vocabulary. A code. He slips under the fallen tree holding the cedar root the way he holds her forearm. He hangs there a moment, his body pulled by water going downriver. Heart Creek? Arm River? he writes, he will mutter to her in the darkness. As his body moves from side to side deliriously out of control, still holding on. Then plunges down, touches gravel and flakes of wood with his back the water closing over his head like a clap of gloved hands. His eyes open as the river itself pushes him to his feet and he is already three yards downstream. He steps into the sun that litters itself now along the whole length of this river.

He thinks of where she might be, what she is naming. Near her, in the grasses, are Bladder Campion, Devil's Paintbrush, some unknown blue flowers. He stands in the shadow of long trees. He has gone far enough to look for a bridge. Turns back upriver. He holds on to a cedar root the way he holds her forearm.

HANDWRITING

parampara—'from generation to generation'

Flight

In the half-dark cabin of Air Lanka Flight 5
the seventy-year-old lady next to me begins to comb
her long white hair, then braids it in the faint light.

Her husband, Mr Jayasinghe, asleep beside her.

Pins in her mouth. She rolls her hair,
curls it into a bun, like my mother's.

Two hours before reaching Katunayake airport.

The Last Sinhala Word I Lost

The last Sinhala word I lost
was *vatura.*
The word for water.
Forest water. The water in a kiss. The tears
I gave to my ayah Rosalin on leaving
the first home of my life.

More water for her than any other
that fled my eyes again
this year, remembering her,
a lost almost-mother in those years
of thirsty love.

No photograph of her, no meeting
since the age of eleven,
not even knowledge of her grave.

Who abandoned who, I wonder now.

In the Sunless Forest of Ritigala

Nine soldiers on leave
strip uniforms off
and dig a well

to give thanks
for surviving this war

A *puja* in an unnamed grove

the way someone you know
might lean forward
and mark the place
where your soul is
—always, they say,
near to a wound.

In the sunless forest
crouched by a forest well

pulling what was lost
out of the depth.

The First Rule of Sinhalese Architecture

Never build three doors
in a straight line

A devil might rush
through them

deep into your house
into your life

A Gentleman Compares His Virtue to a Piece of Jade

The enemy was always identified in art by a lion.

And in our Book of Victories
wherever you saw a parasol
on the battlefield you could
identify the king within its shadow.

We began with myths and later included actual events.

There were new professions. Cormorant Girls
who screamed on prawn farms to scare birds.
Stilt walkers. Tightrope walkers.

There was always the 'untaught hold'
by which the master defeated
the pupil who challenged him.

Palanquins carried the weapons of a goddess.

Bamboo tubes cut in 17th-century Japan
we used as poem holders.

We tied bells onto falcons.

A silted water garden in Mihintale.
The letter *M*. The word 'thereby.'

There were wild cursive scripts.
There was the two-dimensional tradition.

Solitaries spent all their years
writing one good book.

In our theatres human beings
wondrously became other human beings.

Bangles from Polonnaruwa.
A nine-chambered box from Gampola.
The archaeology of cattle bells.

We believed in the intimate life, an inner self.

A libertine was one who made love before nightfall
or without darkening the room.

We aligned our public holidays with the full moon.

3 a.m. in temples, the hour of washing the gods.

The formalization of the vernacular.

The Buddha's left foot shifted at the moment of death.

That great writer, dying, called out
for the fictional doctor in his novels.

That tightrope walker from Kurunegala
the generator shut down by insurgents
stood there, swaying in the darkness above us.

The Distance of a Shout

We lived on the medieval coast
south of warrior kingdoms
during the ancient age of the winds
as they drove all things before them.

Monks from the north came
down our streams floating—that was
the year no one ate river fish.

There was no book of the forest,
no book of the sea, but these
are places people died.

Handwriting occurred on waves,
on leaves, the scripts of smoke,
a sign on a bridge along the Mahaweli River.

A gradual acceptance of this new language.

The Brother Thief

Four men steal the bronze
Buddha at Veheragala
and disappear from their families

The statue carried
along jungle pathways
its right arm raised
to the jerking sky
in the gesture of
'protection' 'reassurance'

towards clouds and birdcall
to this quick terror
in the four men
moving under him

The Buddha with them
all night by a small
thorn fire, touching
the robe at his shoulder,
vitarka mudra—'gesture
of calling for a discourse.'
Three of the men asleep.
The youngest feeds the fire
beside the bronze,
allows himself honey
as night progresses
as sounds quiet and thicken,
the shift during night hours
to lesser more various animals.
Creatures like us, he thinks.

Beyond this pupil of heat
all geography is burned

No mountain or star
no river noise,
                nothing
to give him course.

His world is
a honey pot
a statue on its side
the gaze restless
from firelight

        He climbs
behind the bronze
slides his arm around
with the knife
and removes the eyes

        chipped gems
fall into his hands

        then startles
innocent
out of his nightmare
rubs his own eyes

He stands and
breathes night

air deep
into himself

swallows all
he can of
thorn smoke

nine small sounds
a distant coolness

          Dark peace,
like a cave of water

750 AD

750 AD a statue of a Samadhi Buddha
was carefully hidden, escaping war,
treasure hunters, fifty-year feuds.
He was discovered by monks in 1870
sitting upright
buried in Anuradhapura earth,
eyes half closed, hands
in the gesture of meditation.

Pulled from the earth with ropes
into a surrounding world.
Pulled into heatwave, insect noise,
bathers splashing in tanks.

Bronze became bronze
around him,
colour became colour.

What Can Be Named in the Earth

Thuringite, zircon, arkose,
terra rossa, limestone. Peat
in the Muthurajawela swamp.

Green marble and rare graphite
in their silent darkness.

On sparser maps the few hidden bodies of water.

On the three floors of the zoological museum
at Marcus Fernando Mawatha
mammals evolving through time,
stilled dioramas of wading birds
stalking the river basins,

with illustrations and weak recordings
of how tailorbirds, hill mynahs,
bill clatterers, the drongo
alter their plumage and calls
when migrating north.

Night paths of vampire bats,
unable to see in daylight.

Forests destroyed by leaf-cutter ants,
recordings of altitude and dialect,
contour maps of drought,
                    the sound levels
of recorded thunder.

All data avoids the naming of cities,
rivers, ancient harbours.

There is no evidence of human life
save the rarely visited village
of Maha Illuppallama
whose every hour of rainfall
was for some reason recorded
each day in 1931.

Only at the Nadesan Centre
are there dated political maps
with named mass graves,
the thousand illegal burials.

The Poets Wrote Their Stories on Rock and Leaf

to celebrate the work of the day,
the shadow pleasures of night.
Kanakara, they said.
Tharu piri . . .

They slept, famous, in palace courtyards
then hid within forests when they were hunted
for composing the arts of love and science
while there was war to celebrate.

They were revealed in their darknesses
—as if a torch were held above the night sea
exposing the bodies of fish—
and were killed and made more famous.

Night Fever

Overlooking a lake
that has buried a village

Bent over a table
shaking from fever
listening for the drowned
name of a town

There's water in my bones
a ghost of a chance

Rock paintings eaten
by amoebic bacteria
streets and temples
that shake within
cliffs of night water

Someone with fever
buried
in the darkness of a room

Lightning over that drowned valley
Thomas Merton who died of electricity

But if I had to perish twice?

What We Lost

The interior love poem
the deeper levels of the self
landscapes of daily life

dates when the abandonment
of certain principles occurred.

The rule of courtesy—how to enter
a temple or forest, how to touch
a master's feet before lesson or performance.

The art of the drum. The art of eye painting.
How to cut an arrow. Gestures between lovers.
The pattern of her teeth marks on his skin
drawn by a monk from memory.

The limits of betrayal. The five ways
a lover could mock an ex-lover.

Nine finger and eye gestures
to signal key emotions.

The small boats of solitude.

Lyrics that rose
from love
back into the air

naked with guile
and praise.

Our works and days.

'All those poets as famous as kings'

Hora gamanak yana ganiyak	A woman who journeys to a tryst
kanakara nathuva	having no jewels,
kaluwan kes kalamba	darkness in her hair,
tharu piri ahasa	the sky lovely with its stars

An Old Book on the Poisons of Madness

An old book on the poisons
of madness, a map
of forest monasteries,
a chronicle brought across
the sea in Sanskrit slokas.
I hold all these
but you have become
a ghost for me.

I hold only your shadow
since those days I drove
your nature away.
A falcon who became a coward.

I hold you the way astronomers
draw constellations for each other
in the markets of wisdom
placing shells
on a dark blanket
saying 'these
are the heavens'

calculating the movement
of the great stars

Nights when I drove

from dark rural highways
into a city wild with light
I remember you in a rented car
in blackness, a loose map on your knees
both of us tense with sudden geography

Or in an airport bus after days of solitude
as if returning to this planet from another
with time pushed back into our bodies
only our eyes holding on to each other
with the danger of our love

Life Before Desire

Life before desire
without conscience.
Cities without rivers or bells.

Where is the forest
not cut down
for profit or literature

whose blossoms instead
will close the heart

Where is the suitor
un-distressed
one can talk with

Where is there a room
without the damn god of love?

Death at Kataragama

For half the day blackouts stroke this house into stillness so there is no longer a whirring fan or the hum of light. You hear sounds of a pencil being felt for in a drawer in the dark and then see its thick shadow in candlelight, writing the remaining words. Paragraphs reduced to one word. A punctuation mark. Then another word, complete as a thought. The way someone's name holds terraces of character, contains all of our adventures together. I walk the corridors which might perhaps, I'm not sure, be cooler than the rest of the house. Heat at noon. Heat in the darkness of night.

There is a woodpecker I am enamoured of I saw this morning through my binoculars. A red thatch roof to his head more modest than crimson, deeper than blood. Distance is always clearer. I no longer see words in focus. As if my soul is a blunt tooth. I bend close to the page to be nearer to what is being understood, though what I write will drift away. I will be able to understand the world only at arm's length.

Can my soul step into the body of that woodpecker? He may be too hot in sunlight, it could be a limited life. But if this had been offered to me today, at 9 a.m., I would have gone with him, traded this body for his.

A constant fall of leaf around me in this time of no rain like the continual habit of death. Someone soon will say of me, 'his body was lying in Kataragama like a pauper.' Vanity, even when we are a corpse. For a blue hand that contains no touch or desire in it for another.

There is something else. Not just the woodpecker. Ten water buffalo when I stopped the car. They were being veered from side to side under the sun. The sloshing of their hooves in the paddy field that I heard thirty yards away, my car door open for the breeze, the haunting sound I was caught within as if creatures of magnificence were undressing and removing their wings. My head and almost-held breath out there for an hour so that later I felt as if I contained that full noon light.

It was water in an earlier life I could not take into my mouth when I was dying. I was soothed then the way a plant would be, brushed with a wet cloth, as I reduced all thought into requests. Take care of this flower. Less light. Curtain. As I lay there prone during the long vigil of my friends. The ache of ribs from too much sleep or fever—bones that protect the heart and breath in battle, during love beside another. Saliva, breath, fluids, the soul. The place bodies meet is the place of escape.

But this time brutal aloneness. The straight stern legs of the woodpecker braced against the jackfruit as he delves for a meal. Will he feel the change in his nature as my soul enters? Will it go darker? Or will I enter as I always do another's nest, wearing their clothes and with their rules for a particular life?

Or I could leap into knee-deep mud potent with rice. Ten water buffalo. A quick decision. Not goals considered all our lives but, in the final minutes, sudden choice. This morning it was a woodpecker. A year ago the face of someone on a train. We depart into worlds that have nothing to do with those we love. This woman whose arm I would hold and comfort, that book I wanted to make and shape tight as a stone—I would give everything away for this sound of mud and water, hooves, great wings.

Driving with Dominic in the Southern Province We See Hints of the Circus

The tattered Hungarian tent

A man washing a trumpet
at a roadside tap

Children in the trees,

one falling
into the grip of another

The Great Tree

'Zou Fulei died like a dragon breaking down a wall . . .'

this line composed and ribboned
in cursive script
by his friend the poet Yang Weizhen

whose father built a library
surrounded by hundreds of plum trees

It was Zou Fulei, almost unknown,
who made the best plum flower painting
of any period

One branch lifted into the wind

and his friend's vertical line of character

their tones of ink
—wet to opaque
dark to pale

each sweep and gesture
trained and various
echoing the other's art

In the high plum-surrounded library
where Yang Weizhen studied as a boy
a moveable staircase was pulled away
to ensure his solitary concentration

His great work
'un-trammelled' 'eccentric' 'unorthodox'
'no taint of the superficial'
'no flamboyant movement'

using at times the lifted tails
of archaic script,

sharing with Zou Fulei
his leaps and darknesses

*

'So I have always held you in my heart . . .'

The great 14th-century poet calligrapher
mourns the death of his friend

Language attacks the paper from the air

There is only a path of blossoms

no flamboyant movement

A night of smoky ink in 1361
a night without a staircase

House on a Red Cliff

There is no mirror in Mirissa

the sea is in the leaves
the waves are in the palms

old languages in the arms
of the casuarina pine

parampara parampara
                                        'from
generation to generation'

The flamboyant a grandfather planted
having lived through fire
lifts itself over the roof

unframed

the house an open net
where the night concentrates
on a breath
                on a step
a thing or gesture
we cannot be attached to

The long, the short, the difficult minutes
of night

where even in darkness
there is no horizon without a tree

just a boat's light in the leaves

Last footstep before formlessness

Step

The ceremonial funeral structure for a monk
made up of thambili palms, white cloth
is only a vessel, disintegrates

completely as his life.

The ending disappears,
replacing itself

with something abstract
as air, a view.

All we'll remember in the last hours
is an afternoon—a lazy lunch
then sleeping together.

Then the disarray of grief.

*

On the morning of a full moon
in a forest monastery
thirty women in white
meditate on the precepts of the day
until darkness.

They walk those abstract paths
their complete heart
their burning thought focused
on this step, then *this* step.

In the redbrick dusk
of the Sacred Quadrangle,
among holy seven-storey ambitions
where the four Buddhas
of Polonnaruwa
face out to each horizon,
is a lotus pavilion.

Taller than a man
nine lotus stalks of stone
stand solitary in the grass,
pillars that once supported
the floor of another level.

(The sensuous stalk
the sacred flower)

How physical yearning
became permanent.
How desire became devotional
so it held up your house,

your lover's house, the house of your god.

And though it is no longer there,
the pillars once let you step
to a higher room
where there was worship, lighter air

Last Ink

In certain countries aromas pierce the heart and one dies
half waking in the night as an owl and a murderer's cart go by

the way someone in your life will talk out love and grief
then leave your company laughing.

In certain languages the calligraphy celebrates
where you met the plum blossom and moon by chance

—the dusk light, the cloud pattern,
recorded always in your heart

and the rest of the world—chaos,
circling your winter boat.

Night of the Plum and Moon.

Years later you shared it
on a scroll or nudged
the ink onto stone
to hold the vista of a life.

A condensary of time in the mountains
—your rain-swollen gate, a summer
scarce with human meeting.
Just bells from another village.
The memory of a woman walking down stairs.

Life on an ancient leaf
or a crowded 5th-century seal

this mirror world of art
—lying on it as if a bed.

When you first saw her,
the night of moon and plum,
you could speak of this to no one.

You cut your desire
against a river stone.

You caught yourself
in a cicada wing rubbing,
lightly inked.
The indelible darker self.

A seal, the Masters said,
must contain bowing and leaping,
'and that which hides in waters.'

Yellow, drunk with ink,
the scroll unrolls to the west
a river journey, each story
an owl in the dark.

I want to die on your chest but not yet,
she wrote, sometime in the 13th century
of our love

before the yellow age of paper

before her story became a song,
lost in imprecise reproductions

until caught in jade,

whose spectrum could hold the black greens
the chalk blue of her eyes in daylight.

*

Our altering love, our moonless faith.

Last ink in the pen.

My body on this hard bed.

The moment in the heart
where I roam restless, searching
for the thin border of the fence
to break through or leap.

Leaping and bowing.

A YEAR OF LAST THINGS

Lock

Reading the lines he loves
he slips them into a pocket,
wishes to die with his clothes
full of torn-free stanzas
and the telephone numbers
of his children in far cities

As if these were
all we need and want,
not the dog
or silver bowl
not the brag of career
or ownership

Unless they can be used
—a bowl to beg with,
a howl to scent a friend,
as those torn lines remind us
how to recall

until we reach that horizon
and drop, or rise
like a canoe within a lock
to search the other half of the river,

where you might see your friends
as altered by this altitude as you

The fresh summer grass,
the smell of the view—
dark water, August paint

How I loved that lock when I saw it
all those summers ago,
                    when we arrived
out of a storm into its evening light,

and gave a stranger some wine
in a tin cup

Even then I wanted
to slip into the wet dark
rectangle and swim on
barefoot to other depths
where nothing could be seen
that was a further story

5 A.M.

for Stan Dragland and for Kris Coleman

The wilderness of our youth, an empty barn,
dancing with friends into the small hours,
then daylight and the cars swerving away
wordless into the dawn

It arrives all at once tonight,
not as memory, but like a gift
from forgetfulness,
as a desire can wake you

or this poem
based on the accidental change of speed
in a friend's camera into slow motion.
So now I remember
the rest of our shadows
as we danced, all our heartbeats
under the thunder

and I can speak to you the way
we once sang farewells out of our cars
late at night, when those
goodbyes remembered everything

Definition

All afternoon I stroll the plotless thirteen hundred
pages of a Sanskrit dictionary
with its verbs for holy obsessions,
the name for an alcove
of coin washers whose fingers glint
all night with dark lead, grains of silver

Here root vowels take
an accent at high altitudes

the way dictionaries
speak over mountains

A single word to portray light
from that distant village
reflected in a cloud,
or your lover's face lit
by the moonlight on a stage

Landscapes nudge the dialect.
In far places travellers know
a faint gesture can mean
desire or scorn,
                                        just as
a sliver of a phrase thrown away
hides charms within its grammar

                                        —*A guru*
'someone with a light touch'
derives from that short vowel, alone
and before a single consonant

Wherever you turn
definitions push open a door

The precisely named odour of a man
who is a heart thief

a word for the highest complication
during a play used also for impregnation

Attributes of character
link themselves to professions
—a metal worker, the river merchant,
the Commissioner of Oaths,
the census taker of birds who
continues the medieval art
of whistling,

those who carry bees on their arm
like a dark flame,

the sullen recluse
who was once the author
of a prayer

This word for a pool before a temple,
or *a n s a*—'the shape of a shoulder blade'
as in the corner of a holy quadrangle

*

The ancient phrases
give you the coin of escape
—that epithet for those who return
to broken relationships repeatedly

will row you away from confusion
or remain only for remembrance

This is how deep I was lost,
my darling, in a love so narcotic
I possessed unimpaired splendour
having no other want or wish

What was there before
the warmth of that word
for your shoulder blade,
or that time before we moved
to a freedom from desire?

Mask

The youth in his mask, his hand reaching
off camera as if towards a river,
what did he wish for then?
Almost anonymous, half made, yet that hand flung out
towards some want or discovery,
with so much still to yearn for.

Later someone will charm him
and he will row out to farther depths
following the notes of an unknown bird,
eventually waking in a forest,
asleep against her arm.

Younger he had retreated once from an embrace
and woke later within that desire,
as if it could have been a longer night, an open window.
He remembers it like some unread letter, written long ago.

It was his time without maps.
His only journeys were in books with curious plots,
led by a convict, a railroad saga, or a long-distance love affair
where he'd need always to skirt those ships of Tarshish,
escape the hulks in the marsh country.

Following the hand beyond the camera's reach
in a small café, that partially lived life.
The heart not yet broken or guilty,
everything still under the mask,
the future to be gathered later.
This feather of an unknown bird

left on a desk by a child, or the sketch
of an unfinished blue heart.
But that afternoon, what was his hand reaching for
from the small corner of his world?

A Cricket in Oplontis 79 AD

All that is left here on a baked afternoon
is a painted basket, a painted cricket

The pools of Oplontis gone
along with its vast kitchen
The pipes in the walls like dry veins

Only insignificant things survived
the Vesuvian lava and ash

along with names of one or two craftsmen
who conceived a floor design,
a theatre wall, or this desire
in a woman's back so beautiful
you are held there in sunlight,
the brown of her neck's shadow
upon her own shoulder, then falling
onto her still-unrestored lover
without a hand to reach for her

All day the quiet beauty of these
lost things by someone
who was good at women
or figs or perspective
on a table's architecture
before a garden

Nothing else lasted,
as if these might be the only memory
of ourselves when we are gone

Science and patience excavate with brushstrokes
and a house emerges without masters or slaves

Even then there were men and women
like bad swans coaxing you into deep water
or a bed of grass, your lover in your arms,
that basket of figs. All these fragments
wrested away from lava
to remember the end of a world,
how it all had been

when what they had captured, assembled well,
gave them their name

The Panther Artist, The Master of Loss

Those solitaries who travelled through hill towns,
arrived at a rich house and painted a face
responsive to love, froze the look of one
driven mad by a swan

poured mosaics onto a low table,
gathering the colours of flesh
from joy to helplessness
to clarify the conviviality of death
—that reminder at every building's entrance

One travels into the suburb of Oplontis,
that new villa south of Naples,
is brought in, fed with the servants,
and lauded by them for his famousness

He has recorded the gestures of actors,
evoked the brief want between

man and woman, man and man,
disguising his own name within a corner,

draws the panther, paints a cricket,
then on his hands and knees
makes that skeleton in the atrium
of every household before he leaves

Leg Glance

The dangers of the subjunctive mood
when love affairs are still all coal and smoke

and gestures focus on almost stationary details,
a thistle, the moon, an unexpected thrush

In the basic architecture of cricket (apart
from its medieval tone) is the almost sultry
skill of the leg glance, that involves
'a very short parlay with the head'
as Ranjitsinhji said, misquoting Jane Austen

and not bothering to move
from the path of the dangerous ball

It is how you make a song
out of someone else's rumour
far beyond the boundary

having reached for what is remote,
covert during a tender alliance
like hidden stairs down into a pond

Almost sinless, with no moral or latitude
as at the outskirts of a particular kind of writing

Last Things

'Dante's busy writing, say, the Fourth Canto,
and anything could happen.' —ADAM ZAGAJEWSKI

1. WORK IN PROGRESS

The air in the piazza darkens
around Dante Alighieri
stern, high above us
one hand holding a book,
his nose a dagger
in the blackness

Two nights later I dream
Dante's body is a falling animal,
he crawls out of shattered plaster
a blue rough tongue slithering
from his mouth, as if
at the end of the world
there is this lizard
who will walk up
some staircase in the dark,
a finished book in his mouth

2. THE QUICK

Adjusting her sandal, losing her hair,
the four of us at breakfast. Our storyline
feels almost continuous these years later
as if we are oaks lining the road
of a linear village, or within
a posthumous diary.

Strindberg dying in bed felt his pillow take shape,
heard crickets and birds singing within it.
Everything around him felt alive.
Or Agha Shahid Ali before his death
writing in a ghazal,
'Before the palaver ends, hear the sparrows' songs,
The quick quick quick, O the quick of it all.'

3. BELOW DANTE

I had been alone for weeks when we met there,
below Dante. The three of us lounged in a *pensione,*
I was writing a book about a dying man.
Twenty years later, you were in a bed,
on Brunswick Avenue. And I kissed your feet,
Connie, one of my shy farewells.

It was your year of last things,
but you were luminous,
within those final fires.

Earlier, alone in that city, I had dreamed
the statue falling brutal from its noble height,
and the poet crawling through plaster,
so near to where we met
in that piazza those years ago.

Now we gather our days together—
the countless meals, laughter and argument,
four of us at vicious canasta
(those small and essential feints),
margaritas, the dancing, and once
drunk in a car on some island or other,
all those small recalls of this and that
before our walk up a staircase into the dark.

for Connie and Leon Rooke, Florence, Spring 1988
—Toronto, Nuit Blanche, October 2008

Dark Garden

What was the month you stepped, barefooted
(a rabbit's cage fallen open on the grass
below your gaze) onto a nail.
A winter month in the tropics. One of your daughters
recently born. This is all I know of the story.

Not your gasp, or the half collapse
whatever that month was, or even the year.

Where was I in the late sixties?
Somewhere in the middle of a book,
a western with distant violence, and
Sallie Chisum stepping barefoot onto a porch
with Billy to pull a splinter out of her heel.

That faraway echo and coincidence.

So I did not hear the gasp, see her stillness,
or her unheld in that dark garden
during the collapse of everything, a marriage,
no ointment in the house, the children

unawakened, unaware
on that December or perhaps April night
when the darkness took *forever* to die.

Where is that unmarked calendar for 1969
when she cleaned her blood off the mat floor.
A single mother in those missed years,
with only the small glimmer of possibility or luck
still years away from us.

Unlit Hut

Scholar masters of Japan, once samurai,
lived recluse, almost unreadable
in their compassionate gaze

They built isolated huts
with old war blades
and memories of distant battles—
those wounds like sleeve openings
that left unspoken shadows

It was the era of poets
as still undiscovered pathways,
not a song maker among them

They would plot a garden with seeds
gathered during travels,
their first broadcast flung into the dark

then listened within that unlit hut
to what hovered out there

All night a samurai alertness,
the stillness learned
as a boy from an owl,
holding the pulse of that garden
in his ink brush, to bring
what was there onto the page

It was a time when the subject of poems was love
when not in love, with women collaged out of the past

and recalled in a four-line gaze,
a song without shadows, as if
they had sauntered into life
for only a moment,
                                        to be sketched
—a woman walking to the right
while glancing slyly left

the way a forester's child might stumble on
and remember just one
melody of cicadas,
or a poet hurriedly retire a verse with
                                        pitch black / sumac

They were busy with memory,
chanting poems while ill, making fun
of the nightingale, listening to
a night rain worrying the flowers,

or that bell in a Zen temple
'sung by pine and cedar'

Elsewhere a crowded age, prodigal with gossip
against solitary writers—like that one-armed poet
drowned in the river with a lightning bug
clutched in his grasp,
                                        or those Drunken Immortals
portrayed in the style of 'the trembling brush'

But there was also now and then
a walk into a masterpiece
of accident—a nun composing

The well rope has been
captured by morning glories—
I will borrow water

A few syllables from the past

'Some things I just covet,' my friend says
when I show this to her
three hundred years later

A Master of Go

During a formal meeting the writer remained silent
beside the actress, recalling instead that movement
where Ōtake had played Black 67. (It appears
in his short book about truth from a distance.)
Ōtake of the Seventh Rank against Sushei the Master
who was sixty-seven years old by the Oriental count.
Kawabata had been their 'battle recorder.'

'You must leave now,' the actress said.
She had known stage lights, singers, the repetitions
of love. It was the way fame echoed against her.
Whereas he knew books, where musicians
would use silence to enter a home—pausing to whisper
in the forecourt, a double bass carried
with care so not a throb was heard—
following the unwritten law that serenades
should only be heard suddenly, with surprise,
the way he had seen White move from A3
diagonally down like a spy against Black forces.
So she might wake in darkness with a lover,
or even an unknown guest, a song in her ear.

He had heard a writer once remark, 'I like order,
but I like it invisible.' Now his
thoughtfulness was only for himself,
as waiting for Black to play
he spoke of eel restaurants in Atami.

There were still episodes to recall back into his life.
How as a boy he saw electricity for the first time,
or witnessed the sound of weeping.

Youth remembers those unaccompanied moments
—the way a friend, looking back from the sea, could identify
his childhood village to keep the boy he once was in view.

As perhaps years later he himself might witness
a lovers' dawn and farewell all in one, their eyes
forbidding mourning, each instead recalling
the larger landscape of their lives.

It was the day before the test run on the new Itō railway line.

The Geography Sixth

We were the unselected ones, mynahs in our youth,
kept from certain classrooms without knowledge
of what was taught there—the complex sciences,
foreign novels, even rhetoric and courtesy
that might help on some future afternoon
within the corridors of power.

While we were stalled in 'The Geography Sixth' studying
floodplains, maps of far pilgrimages, coastal profiles
of islands drawn by mariners in earlier times.

Still I made my best friends there, in that class
where we talked without pause and with no fear
of boredom. David Gearon, Stuart Blackler,
Geoff Maile, Jeremy Bottle—all my sad captains
raucous beyond midnight
at that wise age of seventeen.

In retrospect we were only discovering ourselves,
immersing ourselves in unnecessary things—
hard-boiled thrillers, how to tap a phone,
the rag-and-bone blues of Radio Luxembourg.
We slipped from school into a dark field,
drank from a bottle, rode a loose horse, and were thrown,
while R B (name withheld) hoisted his Chinese girlfriend,
a composer's only daughter, on a rope
up to his second-floor dormitory, her slipper
floating to earth.

It would be a decade, though it felt just a weekend,
before I stood in front of a Fragonard in the Wallace Collection,

its rapid brushwork of the woman's dress on a swing
reminding me of their quiet whispers as they plotted her ascent,
then noticed that shoe in mid-air, leaving her right foot.
The lighter genius of Fragonard.

It was some time before we were drawn to erotic pleasures
and the disguises of clothing. 'A long dove-grey shirt'
on an 'idle bride' in a mountaineering thriller, that 'air-blue gown'
in a stanza of Hardy, those evolving disguises of the Count
of Monte Cristo, or in the way Stendhal owned 350 pseudonyms
for he disliked the first-person pronoun.

It was now escape from our contained lives that obsessed us
as when Julien in *The Red and the Black* leapt
from a wife's window during an interrupted seduction
into the dark and was chased by friendly guard dogs
who knew him well (that wonderful detail)
'while a husband's bullets whistled past him.'
'You close a perfect chapter and it sounds like a gunshot,'
I read in a Polish essay and knew where it came from.

We were witnessing how characters evolved
from a fragment to become assured though
more damaged, revealed but better hidden.
Youth never remains a sentence.
Even if some were pulled by thick ropes
into dormitories, while others, thrown by the horse, lay
drunk on the grass, without hope of a significant life.

And yet with those dutiful maps of pilgrimages had come
the sudden discoveries of unnamed islands. Though we still
had no idea whether we might leap up or down
into a further story.

Wanderer

Let us speak about our enormous flaws as told to us
by others—accountants, wives before leaving—
about how we deceived ourselves, even our dogs
by ignoring their concerned pre-walk, tear-stained howls,
though they rested often on our chests
making sounds like old ships.

For there is only, but *always,* a small tunnel of escape
for forgiveness. As with any novel or film you hang
onto 'character rights' and where you came from.
There's not much to leave when you're only fifteen, we are told.

My friend's family in Warsaw during the war
was fed and kept alive by a German deserter
who roamed Europe like Odysseus, even
joining them in their escape, pretending to be mute
while they taught him Polish. A dissolved genealogy
let him cross borders and war zones with them,
finding a path through various armies.
He knew already *the great engines of this world*
do not run on faithfulness.

Without a homeland he was for a while
a father to the children.

And later, more than once needing a passport,
he married more than once.

With dialects and port-accented verbs
he could sing in four languages about departure.

He belonged still to himself at fifteen,
waiting for the later years to reach him.

Who had he become? He'd bunked beside Isaiah,
escaped judgement, remained as if impenitent.
He felt comforted only when—as with the dog—
it became difficult to know if accusations
meant damnation or contentment.

November

Where is my dear sixteen-year-old cat
I wish to carry upstairs in my arms
looking up at me and thinking
be careful, dear human

Sixteen years. How many days since
I found you as if an urchin in a snowstorm

and you moved in assured
learned the territories of the house
and what became your garden

Only now do we see the horizon
where you paused two or three times
then slipped into

Was it too soon or too late
that last summer of your life
when we watched your walk
down to a river to take a sip
from its ongoing flow

Oh Jack I miss your presence everywhere
in the corners of rooms, in every chair,
or nesting in a cardboard box

Take me back where the past can again enter
those early remembered rooms, our snowbound street,
lift me upside down in your arms, I cannot stand it

I need a journey too. Have I slept my life away,
do I understand anything? Will I wear a bell
like yours into the afterlife where language
no longer exists and we gather only linked sounds
like oars from a passing boat,
                                        those few syllables
to recall tenderness

You no longer wait for us

All day long, Bashō wrote,
A lark sings in the air
Yet he seems to have had
Not quite his fill

'There are three sounds in the wood this morning'

writes Edward Thomas.
Each day he walks the fields in his journal
beside that narrow river, a one-word hill,
with a pause of space he leaves for any bird call

He is the sentinel of quiet places
where nothing supposedly happens,
as when he arrived at Adlestrop by train
and found nothing there, until he listened longer

'Still not a thrush—but many blackbirds,'
he would write, in his last letter,
near the battlefield in Arras in 1917,
those few days before he died

Stella

This morning before daybreak a thunderstorm

In the last hours before her death
her enemies came. A raccoon, that storm,
the FedEx truck manned by a gentle woman
who'd recently lost her own dog.
Considering the woman who was usually her enemy
our dog perhaps read the grief in her,

just as, the night before, a raccoon
along the fence backlit by moonlight
watched our dog drink noisily from the fountain,
her thin body so thirsty! never sensing
the creature who continued
along the fence and disappeared

So many things to learn, keep on learning
during these last days, watching us
with an awareness that we perhaps
have not learned but shall

Now we are less. How do we become more?

How to die courteous and beautiful
protecting her house, guarding our door

His chair, a narrow bed, a motel room, the fox

Doubt or unawareness in the self-portraits of artists.

The photograph of Lucian Freud embracing a live fox,
his wrist intimate against the heart of the animal,
not caring how he looks, unmirrored.

The way Robert Creeley and Robert Duncan face you
with the gaze of just one man between them.

Rembrandt's *Self-Portrait Wearing a White Feathered Bonnet,*
with a proud bearing. Then *Self-Portrait as a Beggar,*
the self pushed aside.

Zhu Yunming, who after wild cursive fame retired
and let his characters dissolve into abstraction.

Those who photograph their shadows on walls
so direct light will not reveal them,
too much knowledge already of the self.

(Degas wished to be illustrious, not well known.)

'See that shadow on the wall,' Steve Earle sings,
'doesn't look like me at all . . .'

A watercolour of Goethe at a window
his back to us, my favourite portrait.
Or Gladstone making notes during old age,
all his focus on his pen, as if blind to the world.

During his last performance on stage as *le malade imaginaire,*

Molière, severely ill, was made up to look the picture of health.
They carried him coughing blood from the theatre to his home
(Purcell's music heard as they climb the stairs).
Nuns from a convent surrounded his bed,
as actors playing apothecaries had swarmed
round him onstage an hour earlier.
There was no priest to pronounce absolution.
The now-four-hundred-year-old leather chair he sat on
in the theatre that night used since only by actors in that role.

Strindberg in a narrow bed during his illness
could take no salutes in person. They placed
red lamps by his window so torch-bearing crowds
recognized his balcony. Lear-like, he gave
all his perceptions to the world
—swifts, sparrows, foxes—
'There are times when I hear a cricket sing
in my pillow. It chimes and rhymes
all the remaining night, the way
sounds made by grasshoppers
come from under the surface of the earth.'

At the Hacienda Motel in Los Angeles Sam Cooke was shot dead.
'See that shadow on the wall . . .' All those motels and hotels
in literature and song, where X wrote this,
where Y got drunk, where Z overdosed.
The one Hank Williams was driven past, dead already in his car.
The Slavianski Bazaar Hotel in 'The Lady with the Dog,'
where Dmitri imagines their dark but hopeful future.
The Hôtel de ville de Courtrai, where Verlaine shot Rimbaud.
The Casa Verdi in Milan, where retired opera singers were welcome
along with various heteronyms of Fernando Pessoa
in their afterlife.

Evening

That poet you scorned
for retiring when he was forty

then beginning thirty years later
with the same voice and style,
the crack in his life invisible

What he said in youth
and approaching death
having the same breath
that precise pitch
unaffected by time

What a wonder I think now
after all those wars and eras
of love he must have passed through

not one gesture altered
as he wrote, as if he always slept
this way beside her

What could we learn
by leaving the colour blue
for another

Talking in a River

For years we have talked like this in a river
after months away, how we missed each other,
what we discovered or argued over when apart.
Our stories stitched together the lost winter,
and what occurred in February when this river froze
having been abandoned by us.

We are in this usual gathering place, telling stories
that always begin a certain way, recalling a possibly
altered life, as if within the wide liberty of a novel
—where you might trespass into a field during a first chapter,
or board a crowded train and claim this is where you fell in love.
It is how a person might reveal a desire among friends
with no foothold in this river,
only a cloud's reflection holding you up.

Each afternoon the four or five of us break into song.
Chuck Berry's 'Memphis, Tennessee,' Zevon's 'A Certain Girl,'
remembered from an earlier time when none of us knew each other,
when that storm of music had not yet arrived.

Now we are with each other's children
where there might be a sudden embrace
over a sadness, someone's loss.

But on certain nights the river will rise because
of a released or altered lock a mile north of here
and the canoe that rests on rock will rise
with the water and float away, untethered.

You go after it. You swim downstream with a paddle
to reach it, steer it back.

You journey beyond the familiar properties, find yourself
before long in anonymous water, nothing audible from shore,
only the shake of reflection like a breaking word.
Is this a different mood of the Black River?
With daylight there is the disguised location of the stars.
You recall other journeys where you crisscrossed Lanark
or Frontenac County from river to river and entered
the scuttle holes of the Moira, to swim its maze
of underwater rock you shall never find again.
There were so many streams with abandoned names,
their riverbeds wordless. Whereas elsewhere
rivers even described themselves—the wide Missouri,
the Qu'Appelle, 'Who calls?'

You swim into late afternoon. The past more distant,
more alive. One late spring you sensed your way east,
portaging over fields as if through a postwar landscape.
You forget that river's name you came to, where you beached
the borrowed canoe, entered a café and danced with her for an hour
beside a juke box, faithless near that small river whose creeks had
merged, disguising themselves within another river's name.
He remembers her there by that nameless river, long after,
still envious of himself at that time.

All those echoing rivers where we lost or found ourselves.
Who calls? Who calls?
There was the girl by the Clare River, he remembers now
as he swims into evening with the arrival of those stars.

Minnette de Silva inspecting the de Saram House, Colombo
(RIBA Collections)

Afterword

The poems chosen for this collection were written between 1963 and 2023, across decades, and they really do feel like the distance of a shout. They were written before and during and after my novels. Writers at any age are secretive creatures, and they tend towards solitude; but the writers I knew at the start of my writing life in Canada often worked alongside book designers and typesetters at the small publishing houses I first found there, such as Coach House Press, or they had to earn their living teaching, as I did at Glendon College in Toronto, where I was intricately influenced by others who taught with me. During that time, I was also learning much by working alongside writers like Roy Kiyooka and Daphne Marlatt, artists like David Bolduc, or with experimental theatre companies such as Theatre Passe Muraille. It would only be later that I worked with editors such as Liz Calder in London, Sonny Mehta in New York, and Dennis Lee, Ellen Seligman, and Louise Dennys in Toronto.

In those early years I was also discovering my past during journeys back to Sri Lanka, through historians like Senake Bandaranayake, as well as architects like Minnette de Silva who influenced Geoffrey Bawa, and Anjalendran who would go on to design some of the remarkable S.O.S. villages and schools for orphaned children, and the designer Ena de Silva who built an 'inward-looking house' in a crowded section of Colombo. I was influenced too by the remarkable gathering of historical photographs of Dominic Sansoni, as well as the poetry of Lakdhas Wikkramasinha who had died young.

Meanwhile, back in Canada, there would always be the discoveries of new work by writers and artists, which would influence me over the years: from the classic *Beyond a Boundary* by C. L. R. James to the research of the forensic anthropologist Clyde Snow, and the truly remarkable *Lost Time: Lectures on Proust in a Soviet Prison Camp* by Józef Czapski, translated by Eric Karpeles. There were wonders like *The Dream of a Common Language* by Adrienne Rich, *The Blue Flower* by Penelope Fitzgerald, *A Month in the Country* by J. L. Carr, and, later, *Casting Deep Shade* by C. D. Wright—which is almost an epic on beech trees—and the work of Annie Dillard and Dionne Brand. Or I was learning a new craft with Anthony Minghella and Walter Murch, and even the carpenter Bob Jacobs at the Skootamatta River, as well as the crooner Tom Waits. And, always, our close friend Michiko Sakata, who seems to travel everywhere in the world—most recently to visit Yamadera Temple, where Bashō stopped on his journey along The Narrow Road to the Deep North. The influences have been endless! Including that school friend who took the photograph of me while we were hitchhiking in Europe in 1961, which appears on the cover.

I am grateful to Ellen Levine, Tulin Valeri, and Steven Barclay, who guided me for years in this career. Thanks too to Sam Solecki and Griffin Ondaatje.

*

Thank you, most of all, to Linda Spalding, since we met in June 1979, forever.

And to the recent generation—Calin, Lilla, Graley, Finnegan, Gemma, Akash.

*

And for this book in particular, I'd like to thank those at McClelland & Stewart in Canada, Alfred A. Knopf in the USA, and Jonathan Cape in the UK who have been involved with and supported it, including Stephanie Sinclair, Jordan Pavlin, Deborah Garrison, Dan Halpern, Robin Robertson, Rob Shapiro, Kevin Bourke, Pei Loi Koay, John Gall, Jennifer Griffiths, Ashley Dunn, and Channa Ekanayake.

Thank you to Anita Chong, Editorial Director of Fiction at McClelland and Stewart, for all the work she has done for this book.

And thank you to my longtime friend and editor, Louise Dennys, for the time and thoughtful care she has given to *The Distance of a Shout*.

Notes on Sources

Most of these poems were written in Canada and in Sri Lanka. 'Tin Roof' was written in Hawai'i. A few poems have been altered.

The small image that first appears on the half-title page is of a prehistoric Vadda rock drawing from Galkanda, Sri Lanka, which I found in Senake Bandaranayake's *Rock and Wall Paintings of Sri Lanka* (Lakehouse Bookshop, 1986).

Thank you to the writers whose works I have quoted at various moments in this book. The poems 'The River Neighbour' and 'Pacific Letter' hold echoes of the Rihaku–Tu Fu–Ezra Pound poems. They are not so much translations as relocations into my landscape. A line by John Berryman appears in 'These Back Alleys,' and a sentence from the last letter by Edward Thomas to his wife appears in 'There are three sounds in the wood this morning.' Cole Swensen and James Salter are quoted in 'Wanderer,' as is Linda Gregg in 'A Bus to Fez.' There is a couplet by Agha Shahid Ali in 'Last Things.' I would also like to acknowledge Ariane Mnouchkine for her great film on Molière, and Yasunari Kawabata's remarkable work *The Master of Go,* translated by Edward G. Seidensticker. 'A fried egg sandwich at 1 a.m.' is a line from a lyric by Stan Dragland, and lines by Steve Earle appear in 'His chair, a narrow bed, a motel room, the fox.'

The still image of the man and horse is taken from a 1918 short film. Reprinted with permission of Pond5 by Shutterstock.

PERMISSIONS ACKNOWLEDGMENTS

Grateful acknowledgment is made to the following for permission to reprint previously published material:

Graywolf Press: excerpt from "Forget All That" from *Too Bright to See & Alma*. Copyright © 1985 by Linda Gregg. Reprinted with the permission of The Permissions Company, LLC on behalf of Graywolf Press, graywolfpress.org.

New York Review of Books and the Estate of Lakdhas Wikkramasinha: except from "1950–1959" by Lakdhas Wikkramasinha. Courtesy of *The New York Review of Books* and the Estate of Lakdhas Wikkramasinha.

W. W. Norton & Company, Inc.: material from *The Collected Works of Billy the Kid* by Michael Ondaatje. Copyright © 1970 by Michael Ondaatje. Used by permission of W. W. Norton & Company, Inc.

A NOTE ABOUT THE AUTHOR

Michael Ondaatje's writing includes novels, a memoir, a book on film editing, and several books of poetry, including, most recently, *A Year of Last Things*. Among the many international accolades for all his work, *The English Patient* received the Booker Prize and was made into an Academy Award–winning film. Born in Sri Lanka, Michael Ondaatje lives in Toronto.

A NOTE ON THE TYPE

The text of this book was set in a typeface called Aldus, designed by the celebrated typographer Hermann Zapf in 1952–53. Based on the classical proportion of the popular Palatino type family, Aldus was originally adapted for Linotype composition as a slightly lighter version that would read better in smaller sizes. Born in Nuremberg, Germany, in 1918 Zapf also created the typefaces Comenius, Hunt Roman, Marconi, Melior, Michelangelo, Optima, Saphir, Sistina, Zapf Book, and Zapf Chancery.

Composed by North Market Street Graphics
Lancaster, Pennsylvania

Book design by Pei Loi Koay